INCOMPARABLE POETRY

Before you start to read this book, take this moment to think about making a donation to punctum books, an independent non-profit press,

@ https://punctumbooks.com/support/

If you're reading the e-book, you can click on the image below to go directly to our donations site. Any amount, no matter the size, is appreciated and will help us to keep our ship of fools afloat. Contributions from dedicated readers will also help us to keep our commons open and to cultivate new work that can't find a welcoming port elsewhere. Our adventure is not possible without your support.

Vive la Open Access.

Fig. 1. Hieronymus Bosch, *Ship of Fools* (1490–1500)

INCOMPARABLE POETRY: AN ESSAY ON THE FINANCIAL CRISIS OF 2007–2008 AND IRISH LITERATURE. Copyright © 2020 by Robert Kiely. This work carries a Creative Commons BY-NC-SA 4.0 International license, which means that you are free to copy and redistribute the material in any medium or format, and you may also remix, transform and build upon the material, as long as you clearly attribute the work to the authors (but not in a way that suggests the authors or punctum books endorses you and your work), you do not use this work for commercial gain in any form whatsoever, and that for any remixing and transformation, you distribute your rebuild under the same license. http://creativecommons.org/licenses/by-nc-sa/4.0/

First published in 2020 by punctum books, Earth, Milky Way.
https://punctumbooks.com

ISBN-13: 978-1-950192-83-0 (print)
ISBN-13: 978-1-950192-84-7 (ePDF)

DOI: 10.21983/P3.0286.1.00

LCCN: 2020936447
Library of Congress Cataloging Data is available from the Library of Congress

Copyediting: Lily Brewer
Book design: Vincent W.J. van Gerven Oei

HIC SVNT MONSTRA

Robert Kiely

Incomparable Poetry

An Essay on the Financial
Crisis of 2007–2008 and
Irish Literature

Contents

0 · *Overview* · 13

1 · *On Trevor Joyce's poetry and the Celtic Tiger·* 35
1.1 · *On Special Economic Zones in Ireland and China* · 53

2 · *On the financial crisis and the Irish response and the Arts* · 59

3 · *On Leontia Flynn's poetry and glibness* · 71
3.1 · *On Flynn's poetry, Auden, and fascism* · 75
3.2 · *On Flynn's poetry, rhyme, and race* · 83

4 · *On Dave Lordan's poetry and abuse and scandals* · 89

5 · Thought-starting Clichés · 99

6 · Futures · 113
6.1 · The Decline and Fall of Whatever Empire · 125

Bibliography · 141

Acknowledgments

This text is in some ways the polished remnants of a series of rejected post-doctorate proposals to various institutions. It was conceived in Hong Kong, and written in Cork and London. I must start by thanking Michael O'Sullivan and Emily Ridge — without them and the conference we organized together on Post-Crash Irish Literature I would never have written this. I would also like to thank Tom Betteridge, Luke Cianciotto, Jeff Clapp, Ollie Evans, Fergal Gaynor, David Grundy, Danny Hayward, Ian Heames, Sean O'Brien, Christopher Upton-Hansen, and Jo L. Walton for their help, as many of them made direct comments on a draft of this text — comments which I have rarely been able to do any justice to — or provided support in other ways. Many thanks to the team at punctum books, in particular Vincent W.J. van Gerven Oei and Lily Brewer. Thanks are also due to the poets I discuss, many of whom have patiently replied to queries and emails. I would like to thank all my family, in particular my mother, Helen, and my aunt, Anne, for all their support. And lastly, thanks to Nisha Ramayya, who read and reread sections as I worked on them, whose kindness and intelligence is a constant inspiration.

0

What is it like to write poetry right now at this moment in world history? What is it unlike? Or, to avoid comparisons at all, what *is* poetry now? Fascists and an "alt-right" search for platforms, opposed but not often enough; global warming renders laughable our comfortable and anachronistic sense of cyclical change; secular stagnation mocks the entire program of austerity; a frantic media, its profitability untenable, devours and annotates every tweet it can. We could compare the moment to anything from the discount bin of history — why not, right? — whether it be China in the seventh century CE or the eleventh century BCE. A common touchstone for Europe or the northwest is the 1930s in the same region. It was a decade haunted by an economic crisis, a period of decline. Culture is an uncapturable swarm of what living people really do, say, sing, paint, photograph, and write, but our inability to delineate it in total does not lessen the imperative to ask what happens when our nebulous and uneven cultural moment is compared with a sense of doom and panic inscribed into other eras, or brought into contrast with other times and ideas. We need to pay attention to the ways in which those transpositions might in their inadequate commensurations be an impediment to grasping what is at hand, while they nonetheless jolt us into describing how those comparisons fail, and thereby perhaps become reotroactively justified.

This essay is an attempt to describe the ways in which the financial crisis affected poetry in Ireland, and thereby how economics and poetry interpenetrate. I concentrate on poems that take the economic changes which Ireland has undergone in the late twentieth and early twenty-first centuries as their subject matter, poems which ostentatiously announce themselves as attempts to grapple with those changes. I will largely focus on the work of Trevor Joyce, a contemporary Irish poet whose work emerges from the modernist traditions of Irish literature. The predominance of this poet's work in my argument is partly due to the insistent regularity of his engagement with economic vocabulary and concepts. I will focus on the poem "Capital Accounts" and the chapbook *The Immediate Future* (2013). The center of gravity in my argument is Irish poetry and economics, but other poets and other locales are brought into relation with this, including China and Mexico, countries pulled into this orbit to bring Ireland into relief, because these contrasts are what motivate the poems themselves. By virtue of throwing into relief the ways in which our period is like and unlike these places, times, and writings, the texts I look at offer compelling and troubling explorations of our present moment.

As surely as there is a ground for a simile or metaphor, there is a sky which illuminates that ground, without which it would be unthinkable. The differential between the sky and ground of these comparisons is a kind of torsion which speaks to the irreducibility of the *there and then* of the poems I will discuss. It is this sky I want to gesture toward, the ways in which these poems *don't work* and come apart at the seams. Another more blunt way to come at this dynamic would be to say that commensurability and incommensurability are tightly knotted together. Incommensurability describes that which is impossible to measure or compare, that which lacks a common quality on which to make a comparison. Commensuration is a powerful tool because it can render some aspects of life invisible or irrelevant, as when the wage masks or degrades feminized labor through its differing levels of validation and valuation.[1] Sometimes the wheels come off the commensurations in these poems, especially when they are fixed in place, spotted, analyzed. Their commensurations have a tendency to lose their potency, to display themselves as facetious and inadequate, but that is the whole point, that the mechanism comes apart and we can see what is really happening offstage or behind our backs. The torque between the failure of these comparisons and their explanatory power was and remains a spur to active and passionate thinking at every reading of them that has been given or undertaken in public and private, on page or stage. I want to suggest that Irish literature has taken a decisive turn toward oblique explorations of incommensurability in form and content since the financial crisis of 2007–8.

Much twentieth-century American poetry takes the reconfigurations of society under capitalism as its subject matter. The critic Christopher Nealon has argued that this is the case not only of self-consciously radical or left poetries but also centrist and right-wing ones, and this remains relevant to Anglophone literature of the twenty-first century, in particular the poetry in and around Ireland.[2] One could argue that economic consideration have been central to the sphere of literature in Ireland for much longer. At the putative dawn of Anglophone Irish literature, Jonathan Swift wrote the *Drapier's Letters* (1724–25), a pseudonymous series of pamphlets which laid bare the machinations behind Wood's halfpence (a privately minted copper coinage that was believed to be of inferior quality). Writing for an incumbent public sphere with substantial power, Swift argued that Ireland was constitutionally and financially independent from Britain and thereby he contributed to the formation of a national identity in congruence with certain bourgeois interests. Swift looks smug on a Series B £10 banknote, circa 1976–82

---

1 Wendy Nelson Espeland and Mitchell L. Stevens, "Commensuration as a Social Process," *Annual Review of Sociology* 24 (1998): 313–43, at 314.
2 Christopher Nealon, *The Matter of Capital: Poetry and Crisis in the American Century* (Cambridge: Harvard University Press, 2011).

Fig. 1. B Series, £10 banknote featuring Jonathan Swift.

(fig. 1), while James Joyce, safely free from influencing a political sphere in his own day and age, looks a bit less *himself* as he smirks and casts his eyes downward, looking embarrassed, on a Series C £10 banknote, circa 1993–2002 (fig. 2). Every old Irish banknote stamped with the visage of Swift or Joyce was so blatant a manifestation of the synergy between the Republic and its literary heritage that to venture this point as an argument is unnecessary. Since Ireland entered the Eurozone in 2002, these prestigious names ceased to adorn the local currency. But the writers I discuss in this essay are not in danger of having their likeness adorn a currency of wider validity than, say, the Brixton pound or an avant-garde bitcoin, and it would be a great disservice to their work to argue for its special status. It is common for literary scholars to assert the uniqueness of the Irish literary tradition, and this is undoubtedly due in part to Ireland's status as a postcolonial nation-state; this sense of uniqueness is shared with other postcolonial states. As in many nation-states, literature is to the Irish State what casings are to batteries, but I would suggest that in Irish literature the antagonism between the State's role in the crisis and the experience of its lower classes is more acute than in the literature of either the USA or the UK, where it is perhaps easier for writers to occupy a critical attitude to the state. That is to say, as the literary tradition is more intertwined with nation-building in Irish poetry, the impact of the

Fig. 2. C Series, £10 banknote featuring James Joyce.

financial crisis on Anglophone literature is more visibly discernible in contemporary Irish literature.

The typical narrative of the financial crisis is as follows: the global financial crash began with a dip in the subprime mortgage market in the US in 2007 and hypertrophied into an international banking crisis with the collapse of the investment bank Lehman Brothers on September 15, 2008. Many banks were over-leveraged, with high levels of debt relative to their capital, and because bad debt was pervasive, banks ceased lending. To prevent the collapse of the world financial system, massive bailouts of financial institutions followed. For economic historian Robert Brenner, this global crisis was simply a particularly dramatic expression of a decades-long tendency, the *long downturn*. He argues that capitalism's problem is that rates of profitability have increasingly diminished business cycle by business cycle since 1973. The financial crisis of 2007–8 was merely a manifestation of huge unresolved problems in the real economy that "have been literally papered over by debt for decades."[3] Collective profit-seeking behavior under these conditions must fuel bubbles, attempt to turn those bubbles into real economic ac-

---

3   Robert Brenner, "What Is Good for Goldman Sachs Is Good for America: The Origins of the Current Crisis," 2009, 1, https://escholarship.org/uc/item/0sg0782h.

tivity, and then retract, burning certain stakeholders, perhaps banks, but more frequently mortgage-owners, workers, and of course whatever population capitalism dubs "surplus" at that moment. Ireland was the first Eurozone country to enter recession during the crisis, hit by a sudden rush of rectitude from across the pond. But its problems were not simply imported by the disease vector of bad US debt. The Irish economy has its own unique history of development as a colony and then an independent state which led to this situation. Of particular importance here is the nature of the boom known as the "Celtic Tiger."

The Celtic Tiger appeared to be a long overdue catch-up with the rest of the West. After an anti-colonial guerrilla struggle, Irish Independence was declared in 1916 and ratified in 1921, but the newly formed state was deprived of the industrialized north due to the prevalence of Unionists and Protestants in that region. There followed a civil war which excised leftist elements, and the victors of that conflict had to peg the punt to the pound and continue to run the Irish economy largely as a supplement to the British economy until 1978, when Ireland joined the European Monetary Union, and around this time it became better to run the Irish economy as a supplement to the US economy. Of course, this overview is incredibly simplistic and there were exceptions; in particular, from 1932 to 1938 the United Kingdom and the Irish Free State waged economic war, where the Irish Government refused to pay Britain land annuities from loans granted to Irish tenant farmers under the Irish Land Acts in the late-nineteenth century. These payments had been agreed on in 1921 as part of the Anglo-Irish Treaty. The Irish economy was not in a good position at the outset of this 1932–38 conflict, and this imposition of trade restrictions caused severe damage to the Irish economy. After that conflict ended, Ireland remained neutral during World War II and therefore failed to receive any of its economic benefits in the way that, for example, Belfast industries did. After the war the Republic's economic growth remained slow. But lo, in 1958, down from the mountain came the civil servant T.K. Whitaker bearing aloft a plan for national regeneration. Seán Lemass, who was Taoiseach (or Prime Minister of Ireland) from 1959–66, implemented this plan, named First Programme for Economic Expansion, between 1958 and 1963. It involved abandoning the principle of protection and encouraging foreign direct investment (hereafter FDI, which is defined as an investment made by a firm or individual in one country into business interests located in another country). From 1958, then, Ireland was poised to hoover up any FDI it could get. This moment is frequently retroactively praised as the source of later economic growth. In fact, the policies praised for the boom were instigated by Whitaker in 1958 to little effect, because, contrary to neoliberal doctrine, there is no causal relationship between low taxes and economic success. Although Ireland willingly donned the golden straitjacket, the benefits would only come about when rates of profitability declined in the US, and capital fled in search of profitable ventures.

The performative economic artifact known as FDI is a concept taught in undergraduate courses and perhaps it is of little use in a "globalized" economy—after all, in what *meaningful* sense is the money form tied to any particular nationality? Is it the nationality of the individual investor, or is it the company as legal entity? Is it currency, or is it the nationality of the labor force whose expropriated labor power the money *represents*? In the Ireland of the Celtic Tiger and still now, dependence on foreign firms means that there is a high divergence between Gross Domestic Product (GDP) and Gross National Product (GNP) (also called Gross National Income, or GNI, see figure 3). Economists highlighted over-reliance on FDI repeatedly as a major structural weakness in the Irish economic model.[4] Thinking about sociality under certain market forms, Marion Fourcade has asked:

> What kinds of meaning, sentiment, moral predicaments, and social bonds are these performative technologies intertwined with? How do economic artefacts connect to human

---

4   Peadar Kirby, *Celtic Tiger in Collapse: Explaining the Weaknesses of the Irish Model* (London: Palgrave Macmillan, 2010).

Fig. 3. Irish GDP (upper line) vs. GNI (lower line) from 1960s until 2017. Note that this is in current USD (Nov. 2018), i.e., not inflation adjusted, so the increases are more dramatic than they would be in reality. Based on World Bank data, see https://data.worldbank.org.

relationships — how do they change, how are they changed by them, and what do they say about them? What kinds of political representations are the discourses and social technologies of the market entangled with?[5]

These are important questions, and the first poem I turn to, Trevor Joyce's "Capital Accounts," is a poem which tries to answer these questions with regard to FDI, showing us the kinds of meaning which proliferates with high amounts of FDI bloating GDP figures and a prevalent political discourse justifying this as "globalization." The distortions of GDP and GNP produced by FDI can be detected in this poem as well as the effacement of domestic and feminized labor in the measures of both GDP and GNP.

The term "Celtic Tiger" refers to the economy of the Republic of Ireland for the decade or so spanning the mid-1990s to

---

5   Marion Fourcade, "Theories of Markets and Theories of Society," *American Behavioral Scientists* 50 (2007): 1015–34, at 1027.

the mid-2000s.⁶ In the early 1990s, Ireland was a relatively poor country by West European standards, with high poverty, unemployment, emigration, inflation, and low economic growth.⁷ It had failed to separate church and state and the resulting policing of morality in Ireland sharply differentiated it from many liberal European countries. With the advent of the Celtic Tiger, this changed by degrees as Ireland underwent a period of relatively rapid economic growth fueled by FDI, slowly causing corresponding changes in Irish culture. Former Taoiseach Garrett Fitzgerald says that Ireland's ability to "catch up" with its EU partners during the Celtic Tiger years "owed everything to a happy timing coincidence between the period of peak demand by foreign industry for Irish labour in Ireland and a parallel peak in the availability of Irish labour."⁸ Fitzgerald was right to see the Celtic Tiger as a fortuitous conjunction of circumstances, a lucky break. One of the reasons for the peak in availability of Irish labor, Fitzgerald points out, was the entry of women into the labor market. The bar stopping married women from engaging in remunerated labor was abolished in 1973 (and earlier for women teachers), but it took some time for the number of women to rise in the workforce. Tax policies were introduced by the Minister for Finance Charlie McCreevy at the turn of the millennium which were "clearly designed to increase the workforce in order to feed a young and hungry Celtic Tiger," as they favored married couples where both spouses were earning over those where only one partner was working.⁹ International capi-

---

6   The first recorded use of the phrase is in a 1994 Morgan Stanley report by Kevin Gardiner. See Peadar Kirby, Luke Gibbons, and Michael Cronin, *Reinventing Ireland: Culture, Society and the Global Economy* (London: Pluto Press, 2002), 17.
7   Seán Ó Riain, *The Rise and Fall of Ireland's Celtic Tiger: Liberalism, Boom and Bust* (Cambridge: Cambridge University Press, 2014).
8   Garret FitzGerald, "What Caused the Celtic Tiger Phenomenon?" *The Irish Times,* July 21, 2007, https://www.irishtimes.com/opinion/what-caused-the-celtic-tiger-phenomenon-1.950806.
9   Pamela Brown, "Women at Work: 40 Years of Change," *The Irish Times,* June 8, 2013, https://www.irishtimes.com/life-and-style/people/women-at-work-40-years-of-change-1.1420721.

tal relies on gendered ideologies and social relations to recruit and discipline workers to reproduce and cheapen segmented labor forces within and across national boundaries.[10] Once international capital needed a larger workforce, Irish labor was freed up in particular by allowing Irish women to work outside the homestead through the employment of au pairs from the European continent who would get to practice their English in exchange for a wage and childminding. This makes for a suggestive irony given the role that Irish migrant women played in the social reproduction of native workers in the past as maids, nannies, nurses, and care workers in foreign countries such as the US and UK.

Feminized and migrant labor forces are crucial to reducing the high costs of private consumption and social reproduction at the centers of power and privilege. Much of the Irish poetry about the boom celebrates how far the citizens of Ireland have come, revelling in brands and luxuries and new lifestyles even as it ostensibly critiques them, for there is joy too in repudiation. For example, Dennis O'Dricoll's poem "The Celtic Tiger," published in 1999 in *Weather Permitting,* describes the new youthful workers with the following lines: "Lip-glossed cigarettes are poised / at coy angles, a black bra strap / slides strategically from a Rocha top."[11] Lip gloss and cigarettes, the named branding of the "Rocha" top (John Rocha CBE is a Hong Kong-born fashion designer who is based in Ireland), all suggest a commodity fetishism that is deeply gendered. O'Driscoll ties economic growth to shopping and exhibits an oblique fear of feminization in all its forms.[12] This gendered take on the Celtic Tiger is not without

---

10 Aihwa Ong, "The Gender and Labor Politics of Postmodernity," *Annual Review of Anthropology* 20 (1991): 279–309.
11 Dennis O'Driscoll, *Collected Poems* (Manchester: Carcanet, 2017), 187.
12 Cf. Sorcha Gunne, "Contemporary Caitlín: Gender and Society in Celtic Tiger Popular Fiction," *Études littéraires* 37, no. 2 (2012): 143–58. See also Debbie Ging, "All-Consuming Images: New Gender Formations in Post-Celtic-Tiger Ireland," in *Transforming Ireland: Challenges, Critiques, Resource,* eds. Debbie Ging, Michael Cronin, and Peadar Kirby (Manchester: Manchester University Press, 2009), 52–70.

precedent and is important to my reading of "Capital Accounts," written in 2003 and published in 2007.

Another example is in order, this time from literary criticism. The critic Benjamin Keatinge has claimed that during the Celtic Tiger globalization "engulfed Ireland and threatened her sovereignty and survival."[13] The "her" here signals the furtive entry, stage-right, of Kathleen Ni Houlihan, symbol of Ireland, famously deployed in the theater by Yeats and Lady Augusta Gregory to rally young men to Ireland's defense from the English oppressor. Keatinge's reliance on this figure is curious, suggesting that for Keatinge, Ireland must protect herself or be protected, she must retain her *honor*. A more even-handed assessment might tone down the nostalgia, the hyperbole (*survival*, really?), the paternalism, and the austere implication that Ireland should not *succumb* to this economic boom. An increase in wealth is, after all, a slight increase in autonomy under current social conditions. She should not give herself up for money, no — exerting self-discipline, she must avoid base materialism. Well, all feminized subjects must hustle and do what they got to do in the collective hostage situation we currently call everyday life. Corporate growth and dependence on the FDI sector are obviously not good things for most of the world's occupants, but the language in which Keatinge argues for its eschewal is saturated with nostalgia. Keatinge suggests that poets are defending national sovereignty, noting that "several Irish poets have written persuasively about the dangers of consumerism."[14] But consumerism is the mirror image of what is actually happening under capitalism. For Keatinge, tradition, rootedness, and culture are opposed to popular consumerism. Keatinge's essay upholds an all too pervasive common-sense notion that the growing consumerism during the boom years eroded some kind of Irish culture, replacing it with capitalist ideals of the United States.

---

13 Benjamin Keatinge, "The Language of Globalization in Contemporary Irish Poetry," *Studi irlandesi: A Journal of Irish Studies* 4 (2014): 69–84, at 83.
14 Ibid., 71.

Equally, the massive influx of US FDI and the repatriation of the profits that FDI produced do not figure in Keatinge's account. Although the Celtic Tiger is not an economic and cultural shift that one can simply step outside of to judge, Keatinge should be criticizing petty nationalism, isolationism, and globalized capitalism's ills without rhetorically and conceptually relying on nostalgia and blaming consumers for consumerism. If Keatinge's essay is concerned with globalization in Irish poetry and not the globalization of Irish poetry or of poetry in general, I will instead assume that Irish writing has always been enmeshed in world history and has always been concerned with capital, workers, and migration.

The Celtic Tiger had the effect of markedly increasing international trade and cultural exchange, both of which have been central to the project of what hypermetropic commentators call "globalization," hence Keatinge's use of the term. The Celtic Tiger, they say, was symptomatic of globalization of capital but also of labor — an influx of foreign labor. This altered Irish demographics and resulted in expanding multiculturalism in Ireland's towns and cities.[15] The sociologist Bryan Fanning optimistically claims that the mono-ethnic conception of the Irish nation had been disrupted "at least a little bit" by the Celtic Tiger, even after the financial crisis.[16] But in many ways, xenophobia heightened across both periods. A Referendum on Citizenship was held in 2004, and the majority of the public voted to

---

15 Central Statistics Office · An Phríomh-Oifig Staidrimh, "Population and Migration Estimates April 2003 (with Revisions to April 1997 and April 2002)," December 10, 2003, http://www.cso.ie/en/media/csoie/releasespublications/documents/population/2003/popmig_2003.pdf. Multiculturalism is a centrist, middle-class, and disingenuously neoliberal way of naming a situation in which the ethnicities involved are happy to remain as "cultures" (once a year festivals, ethnic cuisine), without having irreducible political othernesses (like traditionalist religion, for instance, or traditions of capitalist resistance, or criminality) and bolsters a globalized capitalist status quo. It signals a vision of globalized migrant labor in which everything works out in an orderly fashion.
16 Bryan Fanning, "Immigration, the Celtic Tiger and the Economic Crisis," *Irish Studies Review* 24 (2016): 9–20.

remove the constitutional right to Irish citizenship for children born to immigrants in Ireland, suggesting that an ethnic nationalism still mattered to many Irish citizens and that a significant portion of the population had a latent tendency toward ethnic chauvinism.[17] In 2005 the CEO of the American technology giant Oracle, a provider of cloud applications and platform services, was quoted in the *Irish Times* suggesting that the Irish should be more open to immigration.[18] The glimmers of a fissure appear in this yoking together of immigration and foreign investment, as if one entails the other, as if the CEO could speak on behalf of immigrants of all classes and phenotypes. Capital is not people, but certain people will suffer for capital's sins. Labor migration and FDI have tended to work together, apparently part and parcel of the same hustle for profitability that is called variously globalization, neoliberalism, and financialization, but the search for new sites of access to cheap labor coincides with the emergence of a global immigration detention network set to administer the movement of bodies alongside the movement of capital. The rise of ethno-nationalist populism which would become clear after the financial crisis across many advanced capitalist countries — a cadre of countries that Ireland likes to imagine it has joined — and the global network of detention centers go hand in hand. In Ireland, the policy of Direct Provision was introduced in 2000, and it severely curtailed the rights of asylum seekers, providing social welfare according to nationality rather than need. Under this policy, asylum seekers are given full room and board, not allowed to work, and given a weekly pittance to live on, while companies like Mosney Irish Holidays PLC rake in rent

---

17 Kevin Denny and Cormac Ó Gráda, *Irish Attitudes to Immigration during and after the Boom* (Dublin: University College Dublin Geary Institute, 2013). See also T. Dundon, M. Gonzalez-Perez, and T. McDonough, "Bitten by the Celtic Tiger: Immigrant Workers and Industrial Relations in the New Glocalised Ireland," *Economic and Industrial Democracy* 28, no. 4 (2007), 501–22.

18 "Celtic Tiger Prosperity and Immigration Go 'Hand in Paw,' Says Oracle's Chief," *Independent,* July 7, 2005, https://www.independent.ie/business/irish/celtic-tiger-prosperity-and-immigration-go-hand-in-paw-says-oracles-chief-25974378.html.

from the government. These detention centers have been compared to Magdalene Laundries and Famine-era workhouses because of the abusive staff, restriction of personal freedoms, and generally callous attitude to human flourishing they present.[19]

Although the Celtic Tiger is generally considered by many historians and newspaper columnists to be a success story for globalization, for economic historians Denis O'Hearn and Maurice Coakley the Irish economy is better conceptualized as a *bridge economy* between the US and Europe. It was not a product of globalization, nor a product of indigenous economic growth.[20] Certain poets and critics know this, and I would argue Joyce is one such. Joyce's poetry is too focused on a *longue durée* to be seduced by the latest labels for historical processes. His work stresses the slow and often imperceptible effects of space, climate, and technology on the actions of human beings over long periods of time, it is populated by kings, fat cats, actuaries, gods, joy riders, slaves, solicitors, and emperors. Because of the long timeframe this juxtaposition of ancient and modern implies, his work can be usefully read alongside the work of Giovanni Arrighi. Arrighi's *The Long Twentieth Century* from 1994 traces the shifts in the relationship between capital accumulation and state formation over a 700-year period. Building on the work of Fernand Braudel, he argues that the history of capitalism is a succession of long centuries during which a hegemonic power uses a combination of political and economic networks to secure control over an expanding world-economic space. Arrighi then tracks the changing fortunes of English and American capitalism, and in his later book *Adam Smith in Beijing* he

---

19 See, for example, Ronit Lentin, "Asylum Seekers, Ireland, and the Return of the Repressed," *Irish Studies Review* 24, no. 1 (2016): 21–34.
20 Maurice Coakley, *Ireland in the World Order: A History of Uneven Development* (London: Pluto, 2012). See also Denis O'Hearn, *The Atlantic Economy: Britain, the US and Ireland* (Manchester: Manchester University Press, 2015). For further suspicion on the usefulness of the term globalization in describing Ireland, see Nicola Jo-Anne Smith, *Showcasing Globalisation? The Political Economy of the Irish Republic* (Manchester: Manchester University Press, 2005).

suggests that the next global hegemon will be China. Chinese economic growth is feared by the West, and some other contemporary poems such as Keston Sutherland's *Hot White Andy* (2005) have drawn on this theme.[21] The rise of European capital during earlier financial empires partly developed through the mercantile trade of riches from the orient, and now the tables have turned as the ostensibly Communist China is poised to become the next global hegemon of the capitalist world-system.

Arrighi has no truck with the term "globalization" because "much of what goes under the catch-word 'globalization' has in fact been a recurrent tendency of world capitalism since early-modern times."[22] It denotes a system in which "governments have little control over their finances and compete fiercely with one another for the favor and assistance of privately controlled capital."[23] There is nothing really new about the contemporary period. Although globalization may name an "explosive growth in world financial markets," it is not "a *departure* from the ongoing process of world-market reconstruction launched under US hegemony in the wake of the Second World War."[24] Nonetheless, for Arrighi, capitalist development is entering an "autumn" phase as American power wanes. The Celtic Tiger was funda-

---

21 Keston Sutherland, *Hot White Andy* (Brighton: Barque, 2005). See also Justin Katko, "Annotated Worksheet on Hot White Andy," *Crisis Inquiry: A Special Volume of Damn the Caesars with Attention to the Work of Rob Halpern & Keston Sutherland,* ed. Richard Owens (2012): 271–98, at 272.

22 Giovanni Arrighi, "Globalization, State Sovereignty, and the 'Endless' Accumulation of Capital," *States and Sovereignty in the Global Economy,* eds. David A. Smith, Dorothy Solinge, and Steven C. Topik (London; Routledge, 1997): 53–73, at 53. "I find myself thinking that it was the financial press that conned us all (myself included) into believing in 'globalization' as something new when it was nothing more than a promotional gimmick to make the best of a necessary adjustment in the system of international finance." David Harvey, "Globalization in Question," *Rethinking Marxism* 8, no. 4 (1995): 1–17, at 8.

23 Giovanni Arrighi, "Globalization and Historical Macrosociology," in *Sociology for the Twenty-First Century: Continuities and Cutting Edges,* ed. Janet Abu-Lughod (Chicago: Chicago University Press 2000), 117–33.

24 Arrighi, "Globalization, State Sovereignty, and the 'Endless' Accumulation of Capital," 53–73, at 54.

mentally an epiphenomenon to the autumn of the American cycle of capital accumulation.

China bookends this essay because of its importance in the contemporary geopolitical imaginary and in Joyce's poetry, in particular "Capital Accounts" and *The Immediate Future* (2013). Born in Dublin in 1947, Joyce has published more than seventeen works of poetry since his initial collection, *Sole Glum Trek* in 1967. This was the first book to appear from New Writer's Press, which was cofounded by Joyce and Michael Smith with the intention of publishing young poets from Ireland and abroad who were not receiving an audience through the few Irish presses in existence at the time. Joyce kept publishing poetry up to 1976 and then was silent until 1995, when *stone floods* came out. His poetry employs a wide range of forms and techniques, from traditional forms to modern experimentalism. Joyce regularly publishes translations and often describes these as "workings" from a given language to emphasize that they are poetic reimaginings in the tradition of Ezra Pound. He has given public readings of his work throughout Ireland, the UK, and the US. Joyce has had a long engagement with China; he taught classes on classical Chinese poetry as part of the Ireland China Cultural Society in Dublin, which led to him giving a paper alongside Joseph Needham and others at the University of Oxford in 1982.[25] Joyce's work with the Irish–Chinese Cultural Society prompted an invitation from the Chinese government to join an Irish delegation on a three-week tour of China in September 1983.[26] During that period, he passed through Hong Kong on his way to mainland China. More recently, he visited Hong Kong

---

25 Joyce was interested in Maoism in his student days. For a rather unsympathetic account of Western Maoism and the '68ers in France, cf. Richard Wolin, *The Wind from the East: French Intellectuals, the Cultural Revolution, and the Legacy of the 1960s* (Princeton: Princeton University Press, 2012). J.H. Prynne is a poet who also works in a Poundian tradition with an interest in China and remains a Maoist to some degree. Cf. "The Art of Poetry No. 101: J.H. Prynne," *Paris Review* 218 (2016): 174–207. Niamh O'Mahony, "Introduction," in *Essays on the Poetry of Trevor Joyce*, ed. Niamh O'Mahony (Bristol: Shearsman, 2015), 11–28, at 13 and 25n3.

26 Ibid., 11–28, at 13 and 25n3.

in May 2016, delivering a powerful reading of several poems including "Capital Accounts," which is a translation of a text by poet Lu Zhaolin (ca. 634–ca. 684). In what follows, I look at the poem "Capital Accounts" to begin to uncover the ways in which economic concerns enter poetry, and I consider how that poem satirizes the Celtic Tiger.

For Joyce, China's history is of extreme importance in worldhistory; as already discussed, for Arrighi and many other economists, it is the next global hegemon. China has only recently entered capitalist modernity, as its countryside only began fully participating in global market dynamics in the early years of the new millennium, but it has always served as a limit-case for conveying the great reach of merchant capital.[27] It has been argued that if whatever it is we currently call globalization had a big bang it was during the 1820s, when a steady, continuous decline in transport cost brought about a commodity price convergence across nations.[28] In 1829, John Francis Davis published *Poeseos Sinicae Commentarii: The Poetry of the Chinese*. He was Chief Superintendent of British Trade in China, working for the East India Company in Canton, and would later become the second governor of Hong Kong. As he expanded the grip of empire and fueled economic growth, he mused that perhaps Chinese poetry could be mined for useful "grafts" that would help English poetry to thrive:

> Fruits of the highest culture may be improved and varied by foreign grafts; and as our gardens have already been indebted to China for a few choice flowers, who knows but our poetry may some day lie under a similar obligation? However small

---

27 See "Sorghum & Steel: The Socialist Developmental Regime and the Forging of China," *Chuǎng* 1 (2016): 13–210 and "Red Dust: The Capitalist Transition in China," *Chuǎng* 2 (2019): 21–281.
28 Kevin H. O'Rourke and Jeffrey G. Williamson, "When Did Globalization Begin?" *European Review of Economic History* 6, no. 1 (2002): 23–50, at 28 and 37.

the prospect of advantage, every scrap of novelty may turn
out to be a real gain.²⁹

Davis's horticultural metaphor is striking: grafting is a technique whereby tissues of different plants are joined to continue their growth together. In this means of asexual propagation the upper part of the combined plant is called the scion and the lower the rootstock, and the success of the joining requires that the vascular tissues grow together in a process called inosculation. Chinese poetry provides flowers in Davis's image, implying that it will be a scion on the rootstock of Anglophone poetry. The major poet to apply these grafts to Anglophone poetry was Ezra Pound, and it is a *consensus mou* that the work of Pound is a significant influence on the work of Joyce. This graft metaphor carries with it a wide penumbra of meanings, many of which are discussed in the poet J.H. Prynne's *Graft and Corruption,* a commentary on Shakespeare's "Sonnet 15" in which he points out that the word graft has meanings which range across labor, syntheses, and corruption.³⁰ In the first section of this book, I will show how during the period of economic growth known as the "Celtic Tiger" Joyce decided to place himself under the obligation described by John Francis Davis: to use foreign graft. Using Lu Zhaolin's poem as a rootstock to an oblique consideration of Irish corruption, Joyce's poem offers a testament to the asexual and sexual indebtedness of the Irish economic boom to foreign investment, foreign graft or *labor*.

Across the world, hip hop and rap offer a unique populist form of critique and resistance, and Ireland is no different.³¹ The African-Irish rap group Rusangano Family have often focused on the struggles of overcoming cultural barriers in foreign lands,

---

29 John Francis Davis, *Poeseos Sinicae Commentarii: The Poetry of the Chinese* (London: Asher, 1870 [1829]): 79–80.
30 J.H. Prynne, *Graft and Corruption: Shakespeare's Sonnet 15* (Cambridge: Face Press, 2016).
31 For a useful overview of the Irish rap scene, see J. Griffith Rollefson, *Flip the Script: European Hip Hop and the Politics of Postcoloniality* (Chicago: University of Chicago Press, 2017), 232–44.

and the group's early website proudly announced that despite their "diverse cultural backgrounds," they operate "as a family unit." Here, the typical family unit is transcended in the name of the family of the musical collective. The bio goes on: "Instead of struggling with the idea of being different, they celebrate it."[32] There is a reasonably simple multiculturalism at work here. In the song "Lights On," released in 2016, Zimbabwean MC God Knows raps:

> I landed in Ireland in 2001
> About the same time that Dre dropped 2001
> Thirteen years later the album's done
> Rusangano presents *Non-national With an Attitude, Volume One*
> [...]
> Where would I be without JME?
> Without knowing he helped me see that I couldn't be anything else but me
> Half Yoruba, half Igbo
> Lyrics like that freed my soul
> Thought I had to be American, thought I had to be English, everything else but Irish
> Before it's the black boy from Caimans school surrounded by white like my Iris
> I just wanted to be Harlem, I just wanted to be London
> I just wanted to be Trench Town, now it's time to be Shannon
> Now it's time to be Limerick, get used to my surroundings
> Where would Limerick be without GAMAK?[33]

---

32 As the American National Public Radio notes, they are concerned with "the human aspects of migration." Kris Ex, "Songs We Love: Rusangano Family, 'Heathrow',' *National Public Radio*, December 1, 2015, http://www.npr.org/2015/12/01/457924848/songs-we-love-rusangano-family-heathrow. See also Rusangano Family, "Artist Bio." Archived at https://web.archive.org/web/20160510161108/http://www.rusanganofamily.com/artist/bio.
33 Rusangano Family, "Lights On," *Rap Genius*, https://genius.com/Rusangano-family-lights-on-lyrics.

These bars are God Knows's *Künstlerroman,* recounting his struggles to assimilate in Ireland (being "surrounded" by "white"), and to find a means of articulating that experience. His initial influences were English and American. In 2001, the year that God Knows arrived in Ireland, the population of Ireland finally met and began to exceed pre-Famine numbers. He alters the gangsta rap group N.W.A.'s name to reflect his circumstances and equally inspirational is JME, an English grime MC. All have "helped" God Knows to study his craft. He plays the white Irish against the white of the sclera surrounding his iris. But he feels the need to use the actual content of their lives, and now opts to embrace Ireland as subject matter, to focus his attention on the life that he actually lives, as the song's chorus puts it. He turns from Harlem to the city of Limerick where he lives. He ends these bars with a rhetorical question: where would Limerick be without GAMAK? Giveamanakick—typeset as giveamanakick and abbreviated as GAMAK—were an Irish rock music duo from Limerick, active from 2001 to 2009. Would it be too much to read something else into this? Gamak is also ornamentation used in the performance of Indian classical music. *Gamaka,* or गमक, means "ornamented note" in Sanskrit, a graceful touch given to a single musical note or a group of notes.[34] In this rap, it might be synonymous with multiculturalism, which is clearly important to the group's self-image or a figuration of God Knows's presence in Limerick. In a wider sense, the Sanskrit scholar Monier Monier-Williams defines *gamaka* as "causing to understand, making clear or intelligible, explanatory, leading to clearness or conviction."[35] We might parse God Knows's question thus as what would Limerick be without immigration, or,

---

34 Gayathri Rajapur Kassebaum, "Karnatak Raga," in *The Garland Encyclopaedia of World Music,* ed. Alison Arnold (New York & London: Taylor & Francis, 2000), 115–35. See also Harry S. Powers, "Mode and Raga," *The Musical Quarterly* 44, no. 4 (1958): 448–60.

35 Monier Monier-Williams, *A Sanskrit–English Dictionary: Etymologically and Philologically Arranged with Special Reference to Cognate Indo-European Languages,* rev. E. Leumann, C. Cappeller, et al. (Oxford: Clarendon Press, 1899), 348.

0

what would Limerick, indeed Ireland, be without the clarity that immigration brings? This question can, I think, illuminate the first two poems I will be analyzing, Joyce's "Capital Accounts" and Flynn's "Profit and Loss," and it remains a concern throughout.

In this essay I will weave discussions of immigration, sex work, financialization, and export-processing zones through my discussion of Joyce's "Capital Accounts." I will then go on in section 2 to give a brief overview of the housing bubble which popped and ended the Celtic Tiger, highlighting that it was seen many years before it burst. I will discuss some prevalent reactions to the crisis and neoliberalism's relationship to aesthetics, and then go on to discuss how Leontia Flynn's poem "Letter to Friends" reacts to it, by amplifying fear of foreignness and talking about W.H. Auden and Iceland. My analysis of Flynn's poem will then feed into my discussion of Dave Lordan's poems "A resurrection in Charlesland" and "Nightmare Pastoral," which I will discuss in section 4 in the context of the Catholic Church's sexual abuse scandals at around the time of the financial crisis. In section 5, "Thought-starting Clichés," I will discuss a novel by Donal Ryan which offers an account of the crisis and helps to contextualize the ways in which some of the poetry I look at handles or returns to clichés. I then discuss Warriner's *Eleven Days,* followed by an analysis of the ways clichés are addressed in poetry by Lordan and Mairéad Byrne. This will lead into my discussion of Joyce's chapbook *The Immediate Future* at the essay's close. In section 6, "Futures," I describe a speech by Bertie Ahern and describe it as an attempt to cast a spell, whereby I discuss some of Joyce's concerns with divination in the chapbook and relate this to pensions and concerns about the future. In section 6.1, "The Decline and Fall of Whatever Empire," I look to the final poem in Joyce's *The Immediate Future* and consider what other critics have said about the reaction to the crisis in Irish poetry. The sections are uneven in length but form an idiorrhythmic whole.

The range of texts I survey is admittedly unusual: poetry and a novel from major publishers, as well as small-press publications of small circulation which are sometimes difficult to find, such as Warriner's *Eleven Days*. However, Joyce's "Capital Accounts" is freely available online as is his chapbook *The Immediate Future*. In contrast, many of *The Irish Times* articles you might follow up on in the footnotes, if you care to, may not be accessible without paying. Although I have focused on the work of Trevor Joyce, much more could be written about every poet I discuss reacting to the financial crisis. And more again could be written on the poetry of Sarah Clancy, James Cummins, Kit Fryatt, Rita Ann Higgins, Fran Lock, David Lloyd, Christodoulous Makris, Aodán McCardle, Ian O'Reilly, Billy Mills, Billy Ramsel, David Toms, William Wall, Catherine Walsh, and David Wheatley, among others. But I have reacted to the poetry that I encountered at the time that provoked a reaction in me.

1

Where Benjamin Keatinge warns against poetry that allows "the language of the marketplace too much sway," Trevor Joyce runs headlong into that language.[1] "Capital Accounts" is a satirical imitation of the foundations on which the Celtic Tiger discourse was built. Although "Capital Accounts" was composed in 2003, it was first published in *What's in Store* in 2007, the year the bottom fell out of the economy.[2] The poem, whose voice moves between languid translationese and fusty bureaucratic terminology, is distressingly attuned to the linguistic and financial dislocations that come with high levels of Foreign Direct Investment (FDI).

The poem is freely available online, and it may be best to consult this before reading further.[3] "Capital Accounts" has fourteen sections, divided by dots, each of which contains between four

---

1 Benjamin Keatinge, "The Language of Globalization in Contemporary Irish Poetry," *Studi irlandesi: A Journal of Irish Studies* 4 (2014): 69–84, at 71.
2 Trevor Joyce, *What's in Store* (Dublin: New Writers' Press; Toronto: The Gig, 2007).
3 A sample of Trevor Joyce, *Selected Poems 1967–2014* (Bristol: Shearsman, 2014), which includes "Capital Accounts," is available online here: https://irp-cdn.multiscreensite.com/12e499a6/files/uploaded/trevor-joyce-selected-poems-1967-2014-sample.pdf.

and eight stanzas. The characters taking the stage include an old woman, prostitutes, men of varying classes. It describes a bustling metropolis, introduces specific buildings, urban scenery, a "financial / district." The opening then declares that on "the street" "you encounter / only strangers" — not just *people you do not know,* but in *Oxford English Dictionary*'s first sense, *foreigners.* In this manner, immigration is inscribed into the poem at the outset. A woman appears who seems apart from the bustle of the streets just described.[4] This old woman is sick of seeing young people in each other's arms, a sentiment which recalls the Irish Leaving Certificate staple, W.B. Yeats's "Sailing to Byzantium." A "hooker" ventures forth to "do trade," we later get a glimpse of the varied clientele of a "hookers' / sweet emporium," including "hitmen," "fat cats," and "[j]oy riders." The presence of fat cats draws our attention to inequality. This boom, like most, was favorable to high-income groups, wealth was consolidated and directed upwards. Later in the poem, police arrive at this brothel and receive sexual gratification, no doubt under threat of direct and indirect violence. Pompous Ministers and Generals are said to believe their culture will last for "a thousand years," against whom the cyclicality of seasons is invoked. Then the focus is on the figure of a man in a meditative state (he is described as "attentive"), who echoes the old woman of section four. Both of them serve as a counterpoint to the sexually active, and younger, arrogant men and prostitutes populating the rest of the poem.[5] The repetition of "fall" in the final stanza also recalls the close of James Joyce's "The Dead" published in 1914, as well as the all-important season of autumn which, for Arrighi, characterizes the state of American hegemony in its late stage.

The scholar David Lloyd notes that Trevor Joyce's trajectory as a poet must be integrated into accounts of Ireland's attempts and failures at capitalist modernization in the 1960s, '70s, and

---

4 Joyce, *Selected Poems 1967–2014,* 11.
5 Ibid., 13–17.

'80s, and with Joyce's own work as a computer systems analyst.[6] One way of doing so would be to think about the relationship between Joyce's working life and his life's work, to relate his curriculum vitae to his poetic practice. Joyce was exposed to programming systems as an employee of the tobacco company P.J. Carroll from 1976 to 1984. Then Joyce moved to Cork and started his second undergraduate degree in mathematical sciences, and then from 1988 as a Business Systems Analyst for Apple.[7] In October 1980 Apple had opened a factory in County Cork, Ireland with sixty employees. During the Celtic Tiger, Ireland became a major player in the IT industry: it exported US$10.4 billion worth of computer services in 2002, whereas the US exported $6.9 billion. Dell, Intel, Apple, and Microsoft set up shop in Ireland because of its EU membership, relatively low wages, government grants, and low tax rates. The Irish government held up several tax loopholes, such as the Double Irish Arrangement, and multinational corporations dove through them. They had to in order to lower their corporate tax liability and maximize profitability in the long downturn (see figure 4). This arrangement was spearheaded in the late 1980s by Apple Inc.[8] Joyce was part of a team running the systems that ran this business, and a Financial Systems Analyst when he left the company

---

6   David Lloyd, "*Rome's Wreck*: Joyce's Baroque," in *Essays on the Poetry of Trevor Joyce*, ed. Niamh O'Mahony (Bristol: Shearsman, 2015), 170–94, at 192n5.
7   Fergal Gaynor, "Still Man: The Human as Unvoiced in the Poetry of Trevor Joyce," in *Essays on the Poetry of Trevor Joyce*, 53–80, at 65 and 79n15. See also Marthine Sartis, "Textual Voices of Irish History in Trevor Joyce's 'Trem Neul,'" in *Essays on the Poetry of Trevor Joyce*, 29–52, at 30.
8   Charles Duhigg and David Kocieniewski, "How Apple Sidesteps Billions in Global Taxes," *New York Times*, April 28, 2012. "In the late 1980s, Apple was among the pioneers in creating a tax structure — known as the Double Irish — that allowed the company to move profits into tax havens around the world." The European Commission has stated that this "selective tax treatment of Apple in Ireland is illegal under EU state aid rules, because it gives Apple a significant advantage over other businesses that are subject to the same national taxation rules" (European Commission, "State Aid: Ireland Gave Illegal Tax Benefits to Apple Worth Up to €13 Billion," August 30, 2016, http://europa.eu/rapid/press-release_IP-16-2923_en.htm).

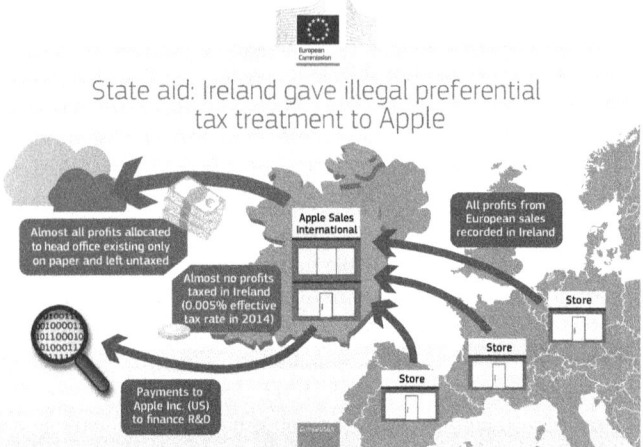

Fig. 4. State aid to Apple. Image downloaded from: http://europa.eu/rapid/press-release_IP-16-2923_en.htm. © European Commission.

in January 2000. The cubicle Joyce worked in for most of his time there was next to that of the Financial Controller of the Cork Plant, Cathy Kearney.[9]

It is worth taking stock here of the period of the poem's composition. In ex-Taoiseach Fitzgerald's view, the Celtic Tiger took place from 1993 to 2001, the year the dot-com bubble burst.[10] The IT industry had over-expanded in the late 1990s, and its stock market equity prices declined sharply. The downturn was partly attributed to the September 11 attacks, which were used to justify a so-called War on Terror. This economic slump lasted roughly until 2003, when the poem was written. On February 15, 2003, vast numbers of anti-war protestors around the world, from Rome to Johannesburg, took to the streets to voice their

---

9 For more on Kearney, see Simon Bowers, "How One Irish Woman Made $22bn for Apple in a Year," *The Guardian,* May 29, 2013, https://www.theguardian.com/technology/2013/may/29/apple-ireland-cork-cathy-kearney.

10 Garret FitzGerald, "What Caused the Celtic Tiger Phenomenon?" *The Irish Times,* July 21, 2007, https://www.irishtimes.com/opinion/what-caused-the-celtic-tiger-phenomenon-1.950806.

opposition to the war against Iraq, which they saw as illegal under international law. A hundred thousand people marched in Ireland.[11]

It would be easy to observe lightly that Joyce's compositional processes are implicated in the trappings of the rise of computing and the attendant economic growth in Ireland — for example, that language has been filtered through Excel spreadsheets and algorithms in the composition of his poems. We can see the use of spreadsheets as a compositional device in many of what Eric Falci terms Joyce's "lattice poems," including *Syzygy* (pronounced SIZ-eh-gee) from 1997, which also features a cold, apparently economic refrain: "we suffer an exposure to the tune of several millions."[12] That "tune" could also mean hearing the voice of the populace at large — millions of people rather than currency. Joyce often highlights his use of compositional procedures and has remarked in interviews that they should be thought about in the context of financial analysis.[13] Without the FDI of Apple we wouldn't have poems such as *Syzygy*. His work, and in particular his use of generative and computerized con-

---

11 Orla O'Donnell, "100,000 March against War in Iraq," *RTÉ Archives*, February 15, 2003, https://www.rte.ie/archives/2013/0215/367908-10-years-ago-today-protest-against-iraq-war/.
12 Eric Falci, "Joinery: Trevor Joyce's Lattice Poems," in *Essays on the Poetry of Trevor Joyce*, 128–54.
13 Joyce writes, "the fact was that I chose these things in order that they might break down, because what I do, for the purposes of the poem, is reduce the world often into a constraint or a set of formal rules which then represent the world and maybe a specific thing within it. I use spreadsheets a lot with the awareness of their background in financial analysis and in banking and such things. It's not accidental that I use them. I was working as a financial analyst in Apple when I started doing it, so it's not whimsical. It's not attention-seeking, although it appears that the most interesting thing a lot of people can find to say about Syzygy is 'Oh, its written using an Excel spreadsheet. Oh, how interesting.' But once I've done that, once I've set up this constraint, then the thing to do is to try to smuggle meaning past or through it, and it has to be disguised in various ways. It will often find itself, if I internalize the thing properly, it will be disguised in ways that even I don't recognize immediately" (Niamh O'Mahony and Trevor Joyce, "Joyce in 2011: Finding a Language Use," *Jacket2*, February 3, 2014. https://jacket2.org/interviews/joyce-2011-finding-language-use).

straints, is tied to the history of financialization of capital and comes out of the rise of the IT industry in Ireland.

Jeffrey Twitchell-Waas notes that "Capital Accounts" draws attention to "the capitalist circulation of money as the primary principle of social relations."[14] But we can press further: poetry is the qualitative practice of what is done quantitatively in accounting, and Joyce's "Capital Accounts" explicitly points to its status as an act of qualitative accounting in its title. After all, a *capital account* is an account that can tell us the net change in ownership of national assets. If multinational corporations based abroad invest in Ireland, this is an inbound flow that counts as a contribution to the *capital account*. This can involve either establishing business operations or acquiring business assets. Through state organizations like the IDA Ireland and Enterprise Ireland, the Irish state attracted US firms in the second half of the twentieth century because of its limited government intervention in business compared to other EU members, and it had cheaper wages than the UK. The Irish software industry was not home-grown, but consisted of foreign companies.[15]

Just as Ireland relied on FDI, Joyce relies on Lu Zhaolin for his poem. In fact, Joyce's text might be read as a subsidiary of Lu Zhaolin's poem. It is a transnational poem about transnational capital. Joyce's scholarly note at the end of *What's in Store* acknowledges that he relied on Hans H. Frankel's book *The Flowering Plum and the Palace Lady: Interpretations of Chinese Poetry* from 1976 and Stephen Owen's *The Poetry of the Early Tang* from 1977 to compose "Capital Accounts."[16] Joyce's poem leans not

---

14 Jeffrey Twitchell-Waas, "Twanging the Zither: Trevor Joyce and Chinese Poetry," in *Essays on the Poetry of Trevor Joyce*, 195–218, at 202.
15 For an optimistic overview of the Irish software industry, see Anita Sands, "The Irish Software Industry," in *From Underdogs to Tigers: The Rise and Growth of the Software Industry in Brazil, China, India, Ireland, and Israel*, eds. Ashish Arora and Alfonso Gambardella (Oxford: Oxford University Press, 2005), 41–71.
16 At the end of *What's in Store*, Joyce attaches a scholarly note to the poem: "'Capital accounts' is worked from *Ch'ang-an: Ku-I* by Lu Chao-lin (pinyin Lu Zhaolin, 635–84). Scholarly translation along with notes, commentary and the original Chinese text may be found in both Hans H. Frankel, *Flow-*

just on the Owen and Frankel translations, but on the surrounding critical exposition of these poems.[17] Frankel tells us that the original Chinese poem "purports to recreate the atmosphere of the Western capital, Ch'ang-an, as it was under the Han dynasty (206 BCE–220 CE)" but is "actually a satire on the contemporary state of affairs in the capital."[18] This capital city was a common topic for Chinese poets of this time and place. Owen notes:

> To the poets of the first half of the seventh century Chang'an excited only wonder; it was *the* city, the marvel of the day, the living proof of Tang power. Being employed there meant or held out the hope of success; being an official elsewhere meant failure.[19]

In Chinese poetry, Chang'an represented the materialistic, aggressive, and militaristic aspects of Chinese civilization.[20] Joyce's title makes the original Chinese much more general—from capital city to capital. This tendency can be seen throughout the poem, whereby Joyce elides any reference to cities at all and also eliminates proper names and allusions, replacing them with his own allusions but never with proper names. This is translation as *transposition* to Ireland. In the title, "Accounts" is plural: there is more than one account. The word accounts might point to the many bank accounts in the capital, that is, Dublin, or the capital

---

ering Plum and the Palace Lady: Interpretations of Chinese Poetry by Hans. H. Frankel (New Haven: Yale University Press, 1976) and Stephen Owen, *The Poetry of the Early Tang* (New Haven: Yale University Press, 1977)" (Joyce, *What's in Store*, 311–12). It is listed in the index of individual poems as "Capital Accounts / (from the Chinese of Lu Zhaolin, for Patrick Galvin)." In *Selected Poems 1967–2014* the poem under the title we are given "Worked from the Chinese of Lu Zhaolin [635–84])" and after the poem "(For Patrick Galvin, 2003)" (Joyce, *Selected Poems 1967–2014*, 18). "Capital Accounts" is the first poem of *Selected Poems*, an order chosen by the poet.

17 In Frankel's *Flowering Plum and the Palace Lady*, 130, it is listed as "Ch'ang-an: An Old-Time Poem" by Lu Chao-lin.
18 Ibid.
19 Owen, *The Poetry of the Early Tang*, 91.
20 Ibid., 92.

accounts of certain companies. It may be a series of narratives or reckonings of Dublin, or of capital itself as money or fixed capital such as buildings. The poem may be an attempt to give a description of some transactions witnessed. The title might be paraphrased as "Money Considerations," "Dublin's Financial Record," "Stories of Dublin."

Joyce's working life resounds throughout this poem. Take, for example, these lines from the second section: "The Corporation's / ornamented halls / rival / the sky."[21] On first exposure, "The Corporation" strikes one as nonspecific, perhaps a specimen of almost cartoonish anti-capitalist and/or anti-bureaucratic satirical language, or a linguistic glocalization. "Glocalization" is the adaptation of international products around the particularities of a local culture in which they are sold, described by Roland Robertson as "the simultaneity — the co-presence — of both universalizing and particularizing tendencies."[22] In the original poem a specific building is referred to — the Liang clan's hall or tower, which Joyce replaces with a more general term, but to those familiar with the Irish capital it denotes a specific building, Dublin's Corporation building.[23] Joyce started work-

---

21 Joyce, *Selected Poems 1967–2014*, 10. In Frankel this is translated as: "The Liang family's painted halls rise to the sky." See also Frankel, *Flowering Plum and the Palace Lady*, 131. In Owen it is translated as "The Liang clan's mural tower rises / into the skies" (Owen, *The Poetry of the Early Tang*, 93).
22 Roland Robertson, "Comments on the 'Global Triad' and 'Glocalization,'" in *Globalization and Indigenous Culture,* ed. Inoue Nobutaka (Tokyo: Institute for Japanese Culture and Classics, Kokugakuin University, 1997), 217–26, at 221. In his contribution, Robertson notes that globalization involves a double movement, both of indigenization and homogenization on page 221. He derives the term glocalization from the Japanese term *dochakuka* on page 224. "The basic idea of glocalization is the simultaneous promotion of what is, in one sense, a standardized product, for particular markets, in particular flavours, and so on" on page 225.
23 The following may provide useful context: "[T]he Liang family, by providing three empresses, became the effective ruler of the country by the middle of the second century, and its members accumulated a vast number of key posts. However, its rivals, the eunuchs, were able, due to their influence on the new emperor, to bring about its downfall, and the whole Liang clan was reduced in 159AD" (Witold Rodziński, *The Walled Kingdom* [Waukegan: Fontana, 1984], 58).

ing at the locally dubbed "Corpo" building for Dublin Corporation's Town Planning Department in mid-1967. The implication of it replacing the Liang clan hall is that the Corpo is the true seat of power in Ireland, an accurate observation in the context of a housing boom which was apparent in 2003. Joyce resigned his permanent job with them in late 1969 to go to college but continued to work in the same building for Dublin County Council on and off until 1975. At that time George Redmond (c.1924–2016) and Raphael Burke (1943–) were active at the Corpo, and Joyce encountered them frequently.[24] Joyce was fired by Redmond several times. Both were later investigated by the Flood Tribunal.[25] In November 2003, the year in which Joyce composed "Capital Accounts," Redmond was convicted and jailed on two counts of corruption.[26] There was also a media storm over Raphael Burke's pension in 2003.[27] Reading the poem in light of these events, the oblique reference to this building takes on great weight. The merger of the original and latter text transposes corruption from the Liang clan to the Corpo in Dublin. Perhaps this is strange, as the poem resides in ambiguity, skirting the accusation of corruption even after courts

---

24 Trevor Joyce, p.c., August 25, 2017.
25 Neil Collins and Mary O'Shea, *Understanding Corruption in Irish Politics* (Cork: Cork University Press, 2000), 28.
26 Tomas Mac Ruairi, "Redmond Found Guilty of Planning Corruption," *Irish Independent*, November 20 2003, https://www.independent.ie/irish-news/redmond-found-guilty-of-planning-corruption-25922956.html; Frank McDonald, "George Redmond among Most Corrupt Officials in Irish History," *The Irish Times*, February 20, 2016, https://www.irishtimes.com/news/ireland/irish-news/george-redmond-among-most-corrupt-officials-in-irish-history-1.2541848. See also Elaine A. Byrne, *Political Corruption in Ireland 1922–2010: A Crooked Harp?* (Manchester: Manchester University Press, 2012), 172–73.
27 Byrne, *Political Corruption in Ireland 1922–2010*, 82–84, 86–87, 170–72, 176–77, 183–82, 221–22, 233–34; Brian Dowling, "Ex-minister on Pension of €66,000," *The Independent*, November 27, 2003, https://www.independent.ie/irish-news/exminister-on-pension-of-66000-25923785.html. See also Paul Cullen, "Review of Report That Made Corruption Finding Against Burke," *The Irish Times*, November 3, 2015, https://www.irishtimes.com/news/environment/review-of-report-that-made-corruption-finding-against-burke-1.2414649.

had ruled that Burke *did* receive bribes. If Joyce's poem avoids drawing too much attention to this, it is probably in order to get us thinking about *structural* issues. The point is not that some people have moral failings but that a certain arrangement of the economy produces certain behavior. The poem, in this regard, avoids making a moral argument.[28]

By section seven of the poem, the Corporation has been renamed the City Hall. It was renamed in 2002, so we could date some kind of transition between sections two and seven to around this time: "At City Hall already / birds / are coming home / to roost."[29] City Hall is getting its comeuppance but we are not told *how*. Owen translates this as: "In the office of the Censorate / the crows cry by night."[30] A Censorate was a high-level supervisory agency in ancient China divided into three branches. One Palace Branch was responsible for monitoring the behavior of officials, another for monitoring the behavior of the emperor, and another for monitoring the behavior of local officials.[31] Frankel translates this as "Inside the Censorate, ravens caw at night."[32] The behavior of the birds at the "Censorate" (translated as "Corporation" by Joyce, as we just saw) suggest that the duties meant to be performed at these buildings are being neglected, an interpretation that, Owen suggests, becomes inevitable as the original Chinese poem continues.[33] Certain systems of regulation are not functioning as originally intended.

This concern with corruption has some proleptic echoes of certain reactions to the financial crisis of 2007–8, in particular the common demand to put an end to crony capitalism. In a discerning essay on contemporaneous struggles entitled "The

---

28 Samuel A. Chambers, *There's No Such Thing as "The Economy": Essays on Capitalist Value* (Earth: punctum books, 2018), 13–58.
29 Joyce, *Selected Poems 1967–2014*, 13.
30 Owen, *The Poetry of the Early Tang*, 94.
31 Wang Yü-Ch'üan, "An Outline of the Central Government of The Former Han Dynasty," *Harvard Journal of Asiatic Studies* 12, nos. 1–2 (1949): 134–87.
32 Frankel, *Flowering Plum and the Palace Lady*, 132.
33 Owen, *The Poetry of the Early Tang*, 98.

Holding Pattern," the research collective Endnotes suggest that in the movements for political and economic change that arose during the time of the Crisis there was a substantial internal tension in this demand, because neoliberalization was a project which replaced "small-scale bribery of officials" with the large-scale bribery of "corrupt privatization deals and public investment projects." Even though neoliberalism presented itself as a movement concerned with opposing corruption, because of the wealth of a certain class and post-crisis bailouts it has come to represent the epitome of corruption.[34] Under austerity, the "limited partnership" in which the poor had been able to enjoy some of the gains of the nationalist project "is being dismantled."[35] We will be discussing this further later in the text, but for the moment it is worth noting that Joyce's poem highlights issues that would become important in the reaction to the financial crisis. The police also feature in the Joyce poem, and "The Holding Pattern" points out that after the financial crisis the police "benefit from an increased access to patronage, even as many other sectors lose such access," and for this reason "the police have become the most potent manifestation, and the most hated symbol, of corruption."[36] It goes on, "rampant corruption means that, at a basic level, one does not really count (or is in danger of not counting) as a member of the nation. What takes the place of a national community is only the police, as the arbiters of the shakeout."[37] The presence of the police in Joyce's poem both highlights and bypasses the issue of community.

In what sense is Joyce's poem a translation, or as the *Selected Works* edition has it, "worked from the Chinese"? It is worth comparing Joyce's version to Frankel and Owen. Each line of the

---

34 "The Holding Pattern: The Ongoing Crisis and the Class Struggles of 2011–2013," *Endnotes* 3 (2013): 12–55, at 37, https://endnotes.org.uk/issues/3/en/endnotes-the-holding-pattern. "In every square, one found signs painted with disgust: corrupt businessmen and politicians had destroyed the economy" (36).
35 Ibid., 40–41.
36 Ibid., 42.
37 Ibid., 43.

Frankel translation becomes two lines in the Owen translation, and in the Joyce translation each Owens line become two lines. In the chronological sequence of three translators (Frankel, then Owens, then Joyce) each typically doubles the lines of the latter, ballooning the poem's length and simultaneously narrowing the poem as it appears on the page. Joyce's rendition is condensed, even blunt, amping up the radical economy of the original verse, an economy (in the sense of excision and conciseness) that has been highly prized in the Western reception of Chinese poetry. In a contrastive description of the differences between English and "condensed" Chinese, Chinese offers "the model of terse fine style."[38] If, for Fenellosa and Pound, poetry is denser with "concrete truth" than prose, then it follows that Chinese poetry is a model of condensation par excellence.[39] Joyce's poem frequently uses the abstracted language of administration presumably spoken in the Corpo building. The languorous and vaguely exotic translationese ("gossamer," "phoenix," "purple mist") is interrupted in the poem by something like a bland brochure advertisement for attracting investment to the International Financial Services Centre (IFSC):

Both the outskirts
and the city's heart
are conveniently situated
just off the freeway,

while major transportation routes
provide immediate access
to the financial
district.[40]

---

38 Ernest Fenollosa and Ezra Pound, *The Chinese Written Character as a Medium for Poetry: A Critical Edition,* eds. Haun Saussy, Jonathan Stalling, and Lucas Kelin (New York: Fordham University Press, 2008), 58.
39 Ibid., 54.
40 Joyce, *Selected Poems 1967–2014,* 15.

As I have mentioned, the main themes of the source text, that is, prostitution and corruption among government officials, are retained in Joyce's poem.[41] Joyce takes these themes and amps up the language, while abstracting from the proper names of the original to what appear to be titles "'Minister' or 'General.'" Joyce translates Owens and Frankel's "courtesans" as "hookers."[42] I need to pause here and take a closer look both at Joyce's act of intralingual translation, or *paraphrasing,* and the two versions in English that he directs the reader to. Here is Frankel's translation:

> Here you come, metropolitan police of the Han dynasty, a thousand horse strong,
> To drink "kingfisher" wine in nautilus-shell cups.
> Silk jackets and jeweled belts are removed for you,
> Songs from Yen and dances from Chao are performed for you.[43]

Frankel's poem addresses the police directly, titillating them with the removal of clothes and mentioning the various geographical regions these courtesans originally come from (Yen and Chao), thereby highlighting that migrating and sex work were as interlinked in earlier eras as they are now. Owen has these "police" as "heralds":

> Royal heralds of the House of Han
>   come, a thousand outriders,
> Kingfisher colored liquors
>   in parrot shaped goblets.
> Blouses of gauze and jewelled sashes
>   are taken off for you,

---

41 Frankel, *Flowering Plum and the Palace Lady,* 135.
42 "And courtesans, pins of coiling dragons, / golden legs bent under." Owen, *The Poetry of the Early Tang,* 94. "Courtesans with 'coiled dragon' coiffures and 'bent knee' golden hairpins" (Frankel, *Flowering Plum and the Palace Lady,* 132).
43 Ibid., 133.

> The songs of Yan, the dances of Wu
> for you performed.[44]

In both Frankel and Owen, the passive grammatical constructions occlude the sex workers while describing their actions: clothes "are taken off for you" or "are removed for you" by unnamed, unnumbered people. The dancers are nowhere but the dance remains as metonym. Joyce's translation definitely ups the sexual overtones of Owens and Frankel while keeping their evasions firmly in place. This is the tenth section of Joyce's poem:

> Now you arrive,
> you civil guards
> of this our state,
> a thousand strong,
>
> to drink
> green wine
> from nacre
> cups.
>
> Gauze boleros,
> jewelled zones
> are stripped
> for you,
>
> for you,
> dance turns exotic,
> and the throat
> grows deep.[45]

Joyce picks up on the repetition of "for you" in both translations and heightens it by putting them one after the other. Joyce explicitly addresses the "civil guards," the Garda Síochána, the

---

44 Owen, *The Poetry of the Early Tang*, 95.
45 Joyce, *Selected Poems 1967–2014*, 15–16.

police force of the Republic of Ireland. The scene described above potentially involves sexual favors being given to police to avoid arrest, hence police abuse. (The Morris tribunal started investigating police corruption in 2003.) Joyce opts for a Spanish loanword when discussing the sex workers — a bolero is a "lively Spanish dance; also the air to which it is danced," but it might also be the gauze boleros or jackets being "stripped" for the "civil guards." The vocabulary in this section suddenly becomes "exotic" just as the dance does, with words like "nacre" and "boleros." This is a poem of foreign workers and foreign words, recalling the "strangers" of the opening section. Joyce's attempt at integrating cold, bureaucratic language and loanwords does not mimic multiculturalism and immigrant integration. The language itself is the immigrant and the prostitute, it is local and foreign, and its "throat / grows deep" for the reader, who is interpellated ("you") as a civil guard. While the civil guards are deepthroated, the "grows" evokes economic growth, but where we usually picture growth as an upwards trend, an increase, this growth is "deep," it goes *down*. Growth and depth are intertwined here, highlighting the predication of growth on debt. This also recalls the name given to the informant in the Watergate scandal, Deep Throat, who provided key details to the *Washington Post*. Corruption is business as usual in both core and peripheral zones.

There is a relationship between gender, capital, and labor at stake here. In 2003 the Gardaí launched operation Quest, which had the aim of tackling human trafficking, prostitution, and criminality within the lap-dancing industry. Many of the women arrested during this operation were not Irish citizens. In one such raid, eighty-one of the 101 held were immigrants.[46] The

---

46 "Minister Defends Sex Trade Raids by Gardai," *The Irish Times* October 2, 2003, https://www.irishtimes.com/news/minister-defends-sex-trade-raids-by-gardai-1.380158. See also Nuala Haughey, "101 Held after Raids on Lap-dancing Clubs," *The Irish Times,* June 7, 2003, https://www.irishtimes.com/news/101-held-after-raids-on-lap-dancing-clubs-1.361662; Eilís Ward, "Prostitution and the Irish State: From Prohibitionism to a Globalised Sex Trade," *Irish Political Studies* 25, no. 1 (2010): 47–65, at 58–60; "Report of

sex worker in Joyce's poem is a migrant, rather than an emblem of the nation Kathleen ni Houlihan, or perhaps we might read it as Kathleen figured as a foreign sex worker. Here, suddenly, the prostitute being pimped to globalized capitalism is not the Ireland of national myth, but a migrant. Who now is the pimp and who the john? Perhaps the pimp is the Irish comprador class? Or the pimp is the system of arrangements which has put the sex worker in this position, with the comprador class as the john?

The IFSC in Dublin is an area exempt from normal taxation laws, dubbed the "Liechtenstein on the Liffey" by Lord Oakeshott.[47] The IFSC is, for all intents and purposes, the City of London's Dublin branch.[48] Even though the poem mentions Dublin's IFSC ("the financial / district"), the only trade actually mentioned is the "trade" of the hookers.[49] This is due to the primacy of feminized reproductive and sexual labor in an era of financialization. Financialization is always tied to the consumption of commodified female bodies. It is not mere coincidence that the IFSC is right next to the historical red-light district in Dublin, known as the Monto.[50] Nonetheless, Joyce's poem par-

---

Department of Justice, Equality and Law Reform and An Garda Síochána Working Group on Trafficking in Human Beings," May 2006, https://www.legislationline.org/documents/id/5371.

47 It was brainchild of financier Dermot Desmond, who approached Fianna Fáil leader Charles Haughey while Haughey was in opposition. Haughey would later lambast the public for "living beyond our means" in 1980, wearing a handmade Charvet shirt. As Taoiseach he engaged in corruption, embezzlement, and tax evasion.

48 Fintan O'Toole, "Liechtenstein on the Liffey: State Policy Has Turned Dublin into a Wild Frontier of Cooked Books and Dodgy Transactions," *The Guardian*, February 27, 2009, https://www.theguardian.com/commentisfree/2009/feb/27/liechenstein-liffey-tax-avoidance-dublin. See also Fiona Reddan, *Ireland's IFSC: A Story of Global Financial Success* (Dublin: Mercier, 2008).

49 "Hookers do trade" (Joyce, *Selected Poems 1967–2014*, 13). For more on the IFSC, see Conor McCabe, *The Sins of the Father: The Decisions That Shaped the Irish Economy* (Dublin: The History Press, 2013), 163–70.

50 Monto was roughly the area bounded by Talbot Street, Amiens Street, Gardiner Street, and Seán McDermott Street (formerly Gloucester Street). The name is derived from Montgomery Street (now called Foley Street),

ticipates in what the scholar Melissa Gira Grant calls the "prostitute imaginary." As Grant says:

> Sex workers' bodies are rarely presented or understood as much more than interchangeable symbols — for urban decay, for misogyny, for exploitation — even when propped up so by those who claim some sympathy, who want to question stereotypes, who want to "help."[51]

The analogies the original poem sets up between these sex workers and corrupt officials are retained, and this is troubling. Joyce is both challenging and reproducing the explanatory narrative of a corrupt state or elite during the Celtic Tiger. The affront embodied by the sex worker, according to certain moral codes, is making sex and money commensurable, which reminds one of Keatinge's moralistic castigation of Kathleen ni Houlihan for capitulating to foreign markets, quoted on page 23 of this text.[52]

The original Tiger economies were the high-tech industrialized countries of Taiwan, Singapore, South Korea, and Hong Kong (later the Hong Kong Special Administrative Region of the People's Republic of China). These regions underwent rapid industrialization, high-tech development and maintained high economic growth rates between the early 1960s and 1990s. All four continue to be categorized as advanced and high-income economies, though they have high degrees of inequality. Hong Kong and Singapore have become world-leading international financial centers, while South Korea and Taiwan are world leaders in manufacturing information technology. The Tiger economies were essentially financialized by allowing foreign female domestic labor to enter the country, for example, Filipino maids in Hong Kong. The Philippine and Indonesian governments facilitated the labor export to assist their economy through re-

---

which runs parallel to the lower end of Talbot Street towards what is now Connolly Station.
51 Melissa Gira, *Playing the Whore* (London: Verso, 2014), 54.
52 Wendy Nelson Espeland and Mitchell L. Stevens, "Commensuration as a Social Process," *Annual Review of Sociology* 24 (1998): 313–43, at 329.

mittances and decreased unemployment statistics rather than building up domestic industry. Nurses and teachers in the Philippines will often leave for Hong Kong, where they earn more as domestic servants. This has a parallel in the growth of human trafficking in sex work in Ireland and in *au pairs* who could be paid a minimal amount and be considered part of a family to mind children, while also having an opportunity to practice their English.[53] The term "Celtic Tiger" exploits a conceptual or historical rhyming between Ireland and these countries. It makes very different things commensurable. The poem presents us with other commensurations, such as its equivalence with a Chinese source text, between the Han/Tang China and Celtic Tiger Ireland, sex and money for the sex workers, and between sex workers and corrupt politicians in the source poem.

---

53 Grainne Cunningham, "How to Hire the Right Au Pair," *Independent,* July 12, 2013. See also Sheila Wayman, "As Employment Rights Change, Has the Au Pair Had Her Day?" *The Irish Times,* January 28, 2017.

1.1

For many, Ireland's loan of Shannon airport to US warplanes was a violation of Irish neutrality, as stated in Article 28.3 of the Irish constitution. One protestor phrased it as follows: "Ireland is prostituting itself."[1] The language of government critique here clearly has some anti-sex-worker overtones. That anti-war movement was also part of an anti-globalization movement. The strippers' "jewelled zones" in "Capital Accounts" recall, though my argument may get a bit precarious here, free trade zones. These zones offer further parallels between economic developments in East Asia and Ireland. Since 2001, the use of Shannon airport by the US military was the subject of protest from anti-war campaigners. It is also possible to argue that this "zone" of Shannon airport, even more tenuously, is where China's rise to superpower status really begins — so compelling is this argument for some scholars that Patrick Neveling says that "it remains to be studied whether the 'rise of the Chinese model' was actually the rise of the Irish model."[2] The first modern free-

---

1 Matt Kennard and Claire Provost, "Story of Cities #25: Shannon — A Tiny Irish Town Inspires China's Economic Boom," *The Guardian*, April 19, 2016, https://www.theguardian.com/cities/2016/apr/19/story-of-cities-25-shannon-ireland-china-economic-boom.
2 Charles Arthur, "A Tiny Irish Town and China's Rise to Superpower Status: The UNIDO Connection," *UNIDO*, March 2, 2017, https://www.unido.

trade zone was established at Shannon airport in 1959, named the Shannon Free Zone, offering companies tax breaks and exemptions on value-added tax on imported goods and goods used for the production of exports.[3] Free trade zones and sites of new industrialization have heavily feminized labor forces, as explained above.[4] Special economic zones (SEZ) would eventually be a major policy prescription recommended to poor countries by the World Bank. The very first modern SEZ was established in Puerto Rico in 1947. But, as Neveling argues, its status as a US colony might have made the model look like an imperial imposition. The Shannon Free Zone is often given the accolade of the first because it is more palatable due to the fact that from the perspective of nation-states it was self-imposed. In 1980, Jiang Zemin visited Shannon as a junior customs official and took a three-week training program on how to set up an industrial free

---

org/stories/tiny-irish-town-and-chinas-rise-superpower-status. Patrick Neveling, "Free Trade Zones, Export Processing Zones, Special Economic Zones and Global Imperial Formations 200 B.C.E. to 2015 C.E.," in *The Palgrave Encyclopedia of Imperialism and Anti-Imperialism*, eds. I. Iin Ness and Z. Cope (Basingstoke: Palgrave Macmillan, 2015), 1007–16. See also Neveling, "Export Processing Zones, Special Economic Zones and the Long March of Capitalist Development Policies During the Cold War," in *Decolonization and the Cold War: Negotiating Independence*, eds. Leslie James and Elisabeth Leake (London: Bloomsbury, 2015), 63–84.

3 Patrick Sisson, "The Small Irish Town That Inspired China's Free Trade Zones," *Curbed*, January 26, 2016. See also "Shan-Zhen: How a Small Irish Town Influenced the Mega-City Shenzhen," *Arch Daily*, January 26, 2016, https://www.curbed.com/2016/1/26/10843212/shannon-ireland-shenzen-china-free-trade-zone. See also Arthur, "A Tiny Irish Town and China's Rise to Superpower Status." For more toothless promises of future trade, see Barry O'Halloran, "Deal with Chinese Province Guangdong Set to Boost Irish Trade," *The Irish Times*, June 9, 2017, https://www.irishtimes.com/business/transport-and-tourism/deal-with-chinese-province-guangdong-set-to-boost-irish-trade-1.3114319. Many economists are lukewarm on SEZs, see more in "Not So Special," *The Economist*, April 4, 2015, https://www.economist.com/leaders/2015/04/04/not-so-special, and "Political Priority, Economic Gamble," *The Economist*, April 4, 2015, https://www.economist.com/finance-and-economics/2015/04/04/political-priority-economic-gamble.

4 Mary Beth Mills, "Gender and Inequality in the Global Labor Force," *Annual Review of Anthropology* 32 (2003): 41–62, at 41.

zone. This training session was one of many organized by the United Nations Industrial Development Organization (UNIDO) in order to share knowledge about the development of SEZs. Shannon Free Airport Development Corporation, a partly state-owned development agency in the Republic of Ireland, worked closely with UNIDO. Under Deng Xiaoping, China was experimenting with opening up its economy and wanted to test reforms in specific areas in the 1980s. China's first SEZ in Shenzhen opened the same year Zemin returned from Shannon. Zemin would become China's president from 1993 to 2003. The Chinese premier Wen Jiabao visited Shannon in 2005.

In Joyce's poem desire for sexual gratification with hookers acts as a social leveler, from poor guys on estates looking for cars to joyride to powerful political elites. The poem levels out these groups of men by virtue of their shared interest in prostitutes.[5] In the poem and in Celtic Tiger Ireland the social is a gendered system of relations in which the male takes pride of place. The poem, like the protestor above, can easily draw on misogyny to deliver its moralizing, by virtue of the content and the wider cultures within which it is situated. Owen says the term in the original poem's title "guyi" might mean "ancient theme/attitude" and in this regard the poem certainly reads as unduly old-fashioned and outmoded.[6] What Joyce's poem highlights is that conditions are made advantageous for such low-tax profits by a pimping elite (low wages, tax rates, etc.) such that foreign domestic investment (FDI) is made to feel welcome in Ireland. But it also highlights that this whole metaphorical arrangement of that understanding of the situation — the pimp (Irish elites), the whore (Ireland), and the john (US FDI in search of a return on investment) — assumes an intranational arrangement to which global capital simply does not correspond, because it makes little sense to talk of capital as though it has a nationality,

---

5   Trevor Joyce, *Selected Poems 1967–2014* (Bristol: Shearsman, 2014), 14.
6   Stephen Owen, *The Poetry of the Early Tang* (New Haven: Yale University Press, 1977), 92.

and the issue isn't in fact corrupt politicians or greedy bankers at all — again, this is a distinction the poem both makes and elides.

The poem is splayed on this constellation of intercultural translation and economics. Joyce reaches back towards Chinese literature to give an account of the Celtic Tiger because of the origin of the term "Celtic Tiger" itself. Joyce depicts this period primarily through imitation: like the label, the poem reaches out to an ideological construct of the "East." The decision to turn to Tang dynasty poetry to discuss the Celtic Tiger mimics the wider economic discourse celebrating Irish exceptionalism in the context of slow European and US economic growth in the 1980s and '90s. This argument, that the Tiger economies function as a justification for turning to Chinese culture, implicitly homogenizes a set of distinct cultural zones under a term labelled "Chinese" or "the East," even as they follow a pattern of uneven development and zero-sum competition. Hong Kong and Taiwan have a complex relationship with China. Hong Kong was a colony owned by Britain and handed back to the Chinese government in 1997, but recent tensions have led to a rise of localists who advocate independence from China for Hong Kong. And, as I finish this, it has become a very large-scale movement and series of violent skirmishes. This homogenizing abstraction is precisely the gesture the term "Celtic Tiger" makes, a remapping that raises questions about using China to analyze economic prosperity and corruption, whether it be through a Tang or Tiger optic. If economic integration "requires commensuration" and commensuration involves globalization and leads to tricky moral conundrums, wherein a foreign prostitute (possibly trafficked) in a vulnerable position is compared to a corrupt government official, we might suggest that the lesson of Joyce's poem is that the commensurations set up under conditions of globalized capitalism (which are also, inextricably, the poem's own commensurations) must be reworked or even abandoned.[7] Joyce's poem is enfolded in the history of the Celtic Tiger, de-

---

7   Espeland and Stevens, "Commensuration as a Social Process," *Annual Review of Sociology* 24 (1998): 313–43, at 325.

scribing it while embalming it in a latent conception of historical cycles, from the Ireland of the 2000s to the Han dynasty and the Tang dynasty. What we have here is a facile globalization, an economic integration that renders disparate times and locations equivalent. These metaphors and conceptual relationships (sexual and asexual reproduction, growth and debt, graft and work, translation and corruption, Chinese and Irish, etc.) are integral to any reading of the poem. The model of grafting and perhaps of hybrid vigor is quite different to the commensurability at the heart of the capitalist project of globalization. Nonetheless Joyce's poetic gesture is quite weird, though its weirdness is extremely instructive — and this gesture maps out a lot of territory other poets dealt with in writing about the financial crisis.

Perhaps "Capital Accounts" is a moralistic attack on overweening pride in any human endeavor, but it might be read better as a satirical exercise in cultural transposition that imitates the discourse of globalization. Joyce's work is a critique of the facile globalization inherent in the term Celtic Tiger even as it is subject to a wider critique of Western claims at intimacy with Chinese poetics. Joyce's poetic globalization is as facile and laughable as the term "Celtic Tiger" itself. The application of the term "Tiger" to describe the Irish economy was an example of facile globalization, based on rendering unique experiences, locations, and practices commensurable; to a large extent this is also the work Joyce's poem performs. The ministers and generals might be objects of ridicule for believing their games will last a thousand years, but Joyce's act of translation and transposition shows that it is apparently not unusual for a poem to last a thousand years and remain relevant to a certain degree. Or perhaps it would be better to say that Joyce's translation not only shows us how little has changed, but all that must be changed.

Fergal Gaynor remarks that this poetry takes revenge on the structures that wield power over the small by invoking the elemental forces of universal change and decay.[8] To the close of

---

8 Fergal Gaynor, "Still Man: The Human as Unvoiced in the Poetry of Trevor Joyce," in *Essays on the Poetry of Trevor Joyce,* ed. Niamh O'Mahony (Bris-

the poem, natural cycles are invoked, including the return of city to nature: "gold steps / and white jade halls / become / green pine."[9] Frankel notes of the original poem that "the constancy of the evergreens contrasts with the inevitable decay of man's costliest constructions."[10] This reading of the original applies equally well to Joyce's translation. The poem, then, oscillates between horizontal relations, upward ambitions, and a contrasting downward movement of the end.[11] It invokes ideas of cyclicality and old age to undercut or temper the overreaching of the ministers or generals. Perhaps Owen's comments on the original poem fit again: "The theme of impermanence here is too meekly universal to be full-fledged topical protest. On the other hand, one cannot miss a general disillusionment with the world of the court."[12]

---

tol: Shearsman, 2015), 53–80, at 74.
9   Joyce, *Selected Poems 1967–2014*, 17.
10 Frankel, *Flowering Plum and the Palace Lady: Interpretations of Chinese Poetry* (New Haven: Yale University Press, 1976), 140.
11 Ibid., 142.
12 Owen, *The Poetry of the Early Tang*, 98.

2

There was a minor downturn in the Irish economy from 2001 to 2003, symptomatic of a global downturn, and at the time many believed that the Celtic Tiger had come to an end. But later virtually every commentator would extend its lifetime to 2007. It was assumed to be the same Celtic Tiger, but in fact the Irish economy pivoted slightly to partake in the global property bubble, and this was clear even in 2003, as the following example shows. On October 16, 2003, the liberal pundit David McWilliams and astringent Austin Hughes (puppet of International Investment Bank at the time) went head to head in the confines of Raidió Teilifís Éireann (RTÉ)'s *Primetime* debate about whether house prices in Dublin would rise or fall. A panel of three prospective homebuyers, Kate Fennel, Jason Ryan, and Patrick Flynn, watched the debate live in the RTÉ studio. McWilliams insisted that rising property prices in Ireland were not reflecting their real value. Hughes pleaded that there was no bubble. McWilliams admonished the panel of prospective homeowners: rent is low, and it is going down. "Keep renting," he said. Hughes claimed that they should "invest now" in property and later "make a return." The presenter Miriam O'Callaghan turned to the homebuyers to see who they sided with. Patrick Flynn said: "We do realize we are in a false economy." What he meant was that everyone knew that the price of houses no longer reflected their value, as McWilliams claimed. Each of the three citizens agreed with McWilliams. They nonetheless said that they would purchase property, before prices rose further. Perhaps they understood better than McWilliams that house prices and rent have a relationship. As Jason Ryan put it, "I don't do a lot on the stock exchange. My house will be an investment."

In May 2007 realtors in Ireland knew the housing bubble would burst.[1] Years of speculation, fueled by the government, bankers, and builders, turned sour. On September 30, 2008, days after becoming the first Eurozone country to enter recession, Ireland responded to the Lehman Brothers collapse by guaranteeing €440 billion of liabilities at six Irish-owned institutions and a foreign-owned bank. With the taxpayers of Ireland as guarantors, Irish banks continued to access loans on the international market. To Europe's irritation, the guarantee provoked similar guarantees across Europe to prevent capital flooding to Ireland.[2] Much of the Irish commentariat have tried to present the later bailout in Ireland as an external imposition, when it in fact followed on logically from this bank guarantee. As the historian Conor McCabe points out, the bank guarantee was the work of "an indigenous middleman or comprador class with business interests concentrated mainly on financial administration and property speculation" that used the full power of the Irish state to protect themselves from their own profit-seeking strategies in the context of a serious crisis in profitability.[3] This class was willing to countenance the financial collapse of the state before they would downsize their houses and lifestyles.[4]

---

1 Derek Brawn, *Ireland's House Party: What the Estate Agents Don't Want You to Know* (Dublin: Gill & Macmillan, 2009).
2 Conor McCabe, "False Economy: The Financialisation of Ireland and the Roots of Austerity," in *Ireland under Austerity: Neoliberal Crisis, Neoliberal Solutions,* eds. Colin Coulter and Angela Nagle (Manchester: Manchester University Press, 2015), 47–65, at 54–45.
3 Ibid., 49.
4 To give context for Irish classes in the late twentieth century, we must look back to the nineteenth century. At that time, Ireland, still a colony, failed to industrialize and was wracked by the Irish Potato Famine. Marx suggested that after the Act of Union in 1800: "Every time Ireland was about

Ireland continues to be dominated by a comprador class which has "positioned itself between foreign capital and the resources of the state."⁵ In October 2008 Finance Minister Brian Lenihan boasted that Ireland's government had delivered "the cheapest bail-out in the world," and it looked like he might be right, because Fitch, the credit rating agency, retained Ireland's triple A rating.⁶ On December 21, 2008, the government said it would inject up to €7.5 billion into the country's three main lenders; Allied Irish Bank, Bank of Ireland, and Anglo Irish Bank. At the beginning of 2009, Lenihan felt assured enough to boast: "The steps taken have impressed our partners in Europe, who are amazed at our capacity to take pain. In France, you would have riots if you tried to do this."⁷ In April 2009 Lenihan announced the creation of a "bad bank" to deal with the risky property loans of financial institutions, taking them off the books of private companies. The National Asset Management Agency (NAMA) was established in October 2009, ready to take on bad assets and loans.

---

    to develop industrially, she was crushed and reconverted into a purely agricultural land. [...] Middlemen accumulated fortunes that they would not invest in the improvement of land, and could not, under the system which prostrated manufactures, invest in machinery, etc. All their accumulations were sent therefore to England for investment [...] and thus was Ireland forced to contribute cheap labour and cheap capital to building up 'the great works of Britain'" (Karl Marx, "Outline of a Report on the Irish Question to the Communist Educational Association of German Workers in London," December 16, 1867, https://www.marxists.org/archive/marx/works/1867/12/16.htm). As Friedrich Engels noted in his 1845 study of the working class in England: "The rapid extension of English industry could not have taken place if England had not possessed in the numerous and impoverished population of Ireland a reserve at command" (Friedrich Engels, *The Conditions of the Working Class in England* [Oxford. Oxford University Press, 2009], 101). Indeed, the Industrial Revolution was predicated on the devaluation of Irish labor and welfare and using Ireland as a source of food.
5 McCabe, "False Economy," 47.
6 Ibid., 53.
7 Anne Lucey, "Europe 'Amazed' at Steps Taken in Budget: Lenihan," *The Irish Times*, April 27, 2009, https://www.irishtimes.com/business/europe-amazed-at-steps-taken-in-budget-lenihan-1.754167.

The newly built Samuel Beckett Bridge, designed by Santiago Calatrava, is modeled on a harp, and the coat of arms of Ireland is a gold harp with silver strings on a blue background known as *Azure a harp Or, stringed Argent*. If you visited Dublin during the crisis and looked through the cable stays of the bridge, named after Samuel Beckett, you would have seen the unfinished headquarters of Anglo Irish Bank, which began to wind down after nationalization in 2009. In July 2011 it merged with the Irish Nationwide Building Society, forming a new company named the Irish Bank Resolution Corporation. Michael Noonan, the Minister for Finance at the time, stated that the name change was important in order to remove "the negative international references associated with the appalling failings of both institutions and their previous managements."[8] The negative associations were also, obviously, local. Anglo Irish Bank specialized in massive loans to a small body of buddies, and the bank and its lendees were central to the overheating of the property market.[9] There is an elective affinity between the bank and what the bridge cannot help but represent, as an immense piece of fixed capital funded by the Department of the Environment Heritage and Local Government, Dublin City Council, and Dublin Docklands Development Authority to the tune of €59.95 million. Both this bank and Beckett exemplify the muddying of failure and success. This link between financial culture (in which risk and failure are perceived as preconditions for profit) and Beckett's writing can be seen in books such as Jean-Marie Choffray and Charles Stephen Brown's *Fail Better!: Stumbling to Success in Sales & Marketing — 25 Remarkable Renegades Show How* (2008), and Pahud de Mortanges's *Ever Invested. Ever Failed. No Matter. Invest Again. Invest Better: Thoughts, Facts and Rules for Learning by Investing* (2017). These texts use a quotation from Beckett's *Worstward Ho* (1983) in their titles, a work of dizzy-

---

8 "Anglo Irish to Change Name as Part of Long Exit," *Reuters*, July 1, 2011, https://uk.reuters.com/article/angloirishbank/anglo-irish-to-change-name-as-part-of-long-exit-idUKL6E7I110Q20110701.

9 Simon Carswell, *Anglo Republic: Inside the Bank that Broke Ireland* (Dublin: Penguin, 2011).

ing negative substitutions in which the "said" is to be replaced by the "missaid," in which "better" is equivalent to "worse" and "well" to "ill." The text is deeply attuned to the constitutive power of language in narrative: "All of old. Nothing else ever. Ever tried. Ever failed. No matter. Try again. Fail again. Fail better."[10] Beckett's work, initially not necessarily categorized as "Irish," has since been recuperated (accurately or inaccurately) during the Celtic Tiger. Remarking on this in 2006, Steven Connor offered a rebuttal to Irish Studies, saying that he did not want to encourage assertions of the "regionality of Beckett's work," i.e., "its 'Irishness', its 'Protestantism', and so on." He observed that "Joyce and Beckett have become the PR darlings of the Celtic Tiger."[11] For Connor, this scholarship is deeply intertwined with the Celtic Tiger discourse and is essentially a branding exercise. Increasingly, nations are acting like corporations. Nation-states are increasingly both cowed under by, and trying to imitate, corporations and firms, as there is "tighter subordination of most states to the dictates of capitalist agencies."[12] And literary heritage for many states is simply one wing of a massive advertising campaign to attract capital.

A close relationship between aesthetics and the economy is a striking feature of neoliberalism, and it is possible to trace this in the language of the reports of the Irish government's Department of Arts, Heritage, Regional, Rural, and Gaeltacht Affairs.[13]

---

10 Samuel Beckett, *Worstward Ho*, in *Company/Ill Seen Ill Said/Worstward Ho/Stirrings Still*, ed. Dirk van Hulle (London: Faber, 2009), 79–103, at 81.
11 Steven Connor, "Beckett and the World," lecture, Global Beckett Conference, Odense, October 26, 2006, http://stevenconnor.com/beckettworld/.
12 Giovanni Arrighi, "Globalization, State Sovereignty, and the 'Endless' Accumulation of Capital," in *States and Sovereignty in the Global Economy*, eds. David A. Smith, Dorothy Solinge, and Steven C. Topik (London: Routledge, 1997), 55.
13 Neoliberalism is a theory of political economy which suggests that human well-being is best advanced by liberating entrepreneurial freedoms with private property rights, free markets, and free trade. The state's role is to uphold this and to create markets. See David Harvey, *A Brief History of Neoliberalism* (Oxford: Oxford University Press, 2007), 2. See also Sarah Brouillette, *Literature and the Creative Economy* (Stanford: Stanford University Press, 2014).

When the International Monetary Fund (IMF) arrived in Ireland in 2010 to negotiate the terms of a loan, the nation let out a long exhalation. After that visit in late 2010, there was an increasing neoliberalization of the Arts sector in which literature was put in service of the economy. A government consultation document published in 2016 on a new National Cultural Framework Policy entitled *Culture 2025* states that "culture creates tangible societal value, promotes wellbeing, and provides a positive direct and indirect economic impact."[14] In the foreword to this document, Heather Humphreys asserts that culture drives innovation and contributes to the "economic wellbeing" of Irish citizens.[15] Similarly, the Department of Arts, Heritage, and the Gaeltacht's *Value for Money and Policy Review of the Arts Council* (2015) notes "the spill-over effects for the economy."[16] This is a marked difference from the Minister for Arts, Sport, and Tourism John O'Donoghue's preface to *Public Art* (2004), where art simply adorns walls of buildings, making "an impact" and creating "lasting memories," and no profit-motive sneaks in.[17] Irish government reports have also commended the cultural sector for responding in "imaginative" and "creative" ways to loss of government funding, and thereby not only is austerity made into an edificatory tool for that sector, but that sector serves as a model student to others.[18] In congruence with this, Colin Coulter has observed that after the financial crisis, academic and intellectual circles were called on to reinvigorate Irish cul-

---

14 An Roinn Ealaíon, Oidhreachta, Gnóthaí, Réigiúnacha, Tuaithe agus Gaeltachta · Department of Arts, Heritage, Regional, Rural and Gaeltacht Affairs, *Culture 2025 — Éire Ildánach: A Framework Policy to 2025*, 2016, 2.
15 Ibid., 3.
16 An Roinn Ealaíon, Oidhreachta agus Gaeltachta · Department of Arts, Heritage and the Gaeltacht, *Value for Money and Policy Review of the Arts Council*, 2015, 2.
17 "Public Art: Per Cent for Art Scheme. General National Guidelines," 2004, 5, https://publicart.ie/fileadmin/user_upload/PDF_Folder/Public_Art_Per_Cent_for_Art.pdf.
18 An Roinn Ealaíon, Oidhreachta, Gnóthaí, Réigiúnacha, Tuaithe agus Gaeltachta, *Culture 2025*, 4.

ture and, by proxy, local apparitions of transnational capital.[19] None of this is unusual or surprising, and it echoes a similar strategy used throughout the Blair years in Britain, which celebrated "Cool Britannia" and attempted to stimulate a "creative economy" in the UK.[20]

In "People & Power — Collapse of the Celtic Tiger," produced by Al Jazeera, journalist Fintan O'Toole says that the arts are immune to the recession. The documentary offers a new gallery space in Dublin, called Block T, "an artistic and social enterprise and a one stop shop for all things creative," as an example.[21] The post-recession mentality is encapsulated by this attempt to turn to the arts as a resource for the creation of material wealth. The ship may sink, but once some coral grows on it, future divers will pay through the nose to behold it. Literature is one of the few places in which misery is itself a commodity rather than a by-product of augmenting commodities. This problem is felt acutely by poets such as Dave Lordan, who asks: "How can we make art from suffering without making that suffering something beautiful and therefore admirable?"[22] Newspaper articles stressed that there has been an uptick in the market for Irish literature and labelled it *post-crash*. The term subtly implies that there is a zero-sum game between cultural and financial capital.[23] The Irish financial downfall is the necessary precursor to a rise in literary quality. Echoing Taoiseach Eamonn de Valera's famous speech during the Anglo-Irish trade war of 1932–37, the

---

19 Colin Coulter, "Ireland under Austerity: An Introduction to the Book," in *Ireland under Austerity: Neoliberal Crises, Neoliberal Solutions,* eds. Colin Coulter and Angela Nagle (Manchester; Manchester University Press, 2015), 1–43, at 18.
20 Robert Hewison, *Cultural Capital: The Rise and Fall of Creative Britain* (London: Verso, 2014).
21 "About," BLOCK T, https://www.blockt.ie/about.
22 Dave Lordan, *The Word in Flames* (2016), 18.
23 Justine Jordan, "A New Irish Literary Boom: The Post-crash Stars of Fiction," *The Guardian,* October 17, 2015. See also Conor Goodman, "New Stars of Irish Fiction: Did 'The Guardian' Get It Right?" *The Irish Times,* October 20, 2015, https://www.irishtimes.com/culture/books/new-stars-of-irish-fiction-did-the-guardian-get-it-right-1.2397659.

underlying assumption is that financial penury is necessary for the land of saints and scholars to fulfil its manifest destiny of stage-Irishness, with fulsome *cailíns* riverdancing at every flyover. This is inherent to the logic behind these newspaper articles and their use of "post-crash" as a term.

A need to write relevant work may be symptomatic of an incursion of economic thinking into the arts. Writers must respond to the conditions under which they write, but the conditions under which they write often foreclose a great many answers. The place of economic discourse in the contemporary Irish cultural imagination has ballooned. It is not a case of writing taking a more important role in everyday life following the crisis but of economics taking a more important role in literature. Consistent attempts to engage directly with economic thought may mean that literature will lose sight of its intrinsic advantage — its ability to handle incommensurables, things which evade quantification and standards of measurement. But literature or writing is probably most useful as a tool when it tries to quantify, and in its attempt renders visible gaps which we must attenuate and break in practice and thought. Its status as an exception to economic imperatives is itself economized and justifies how we all live. Art is posited as a haven for particularity, idiosyncrasy and non-fungibility to legitimate its opposite in the name of a spurious autonomy. Irish literature is engaged in a collective attempt to purge economic language and thought from our collective lives by emptying that language into literature. There is an excessive interest in economics in Irish writing, and this is both symptom and cure, a collective shedding of the economic discourse through overuse. Literature has been funneling capitalism's own image back to itself relentlessly in the hopes that the fumes will damage the car and not the passengers. If literature was suffering, and perhaps continues to suffer, from the pervasive influence of a certain form of economics, we cannot blame the work made under these conditions or the writers. We cannot blame the poisonous gases in the mine on the dead canary. Neither is the dead canary a manifestation of resistance to the conditions in said mine.

On the evening of 1 Frimaire CCXIX the NAMA was established. The Taoiseach Brian Cowen then confirmed on live television that the European Union, European Central Bank, and International Monetary Fund troika would be involving itself in Ireland's financial affairs. Support for the Fianna Fáil party crumbled. In Cork, the poet Rachel Warriner was writing a breath-taking sequence entitled *Eleven Days* (which we will return to in section 5) and attended an anti-IMF protest. On November 28, 2010, the European Union, International Monetary Fund and the Irish state agreed to a €85 billion rescue deal made up of €22.5 billion from the IMF, €22.5 billion from the European Financial Stability Facility, €17.5 billion from the Irish sovereign National Pension Reserve Fund and bilateral loans from the United Kingdom, Denmark, and Sweden.[24] When the IMF arrived in Ireland in 2010 to negotiate the terms of a loan, a major Irish newspaper editorial articulated the outrage of the petty bourgeoisie by opining that Ireland's freedom fighters had died for nothing, taking a quotation from W.B. Yeats's "September 1913" as a title for their lament: "Was it for this…?" Utilizing this poem, which meditates upon Ireland's revolution and nationalist movement at the beginning of the twentieth century, the editorial suggested that Ireland's revolutionaries died for national sovereignty, only to have it given to German banks. The *Irish Times* editorial stated:

> The true ignominy of our current situation is not that our sovereignty has been taken away from us, it is that we ourselves have squandered it. Let us not seek to assuage our sense of shame in the comforting illusion that powerful nations in Europe are conspiring to become our masters. We are, after all, no great prize for any would-be overlord now. No rational European would willingly take on the task of cleaning up the

---

24 Lisa O'Carroll, "Government Statement on the announcement of joint EU–IMF Programme for Ireland," *The Guardian*, November 28, 2010. "Eurozone Agrees €85bn Deal for Ireland," RTÉ, November 29, 2010, https://www.rte.ie/news/2010/1128/294894-economy/.

mess we have made. It is the incompetence of the governments we ourselves elected that has so deeply compromised our capacity to make our own decisions.

They did so, let us recall, from a period when Irish sovereignty had never been stronger. Our national debt was negligible. The mass emigration that had mocked our claims to be a people in control of our own destiny was reversed. A genuine act of national self-determination had occurred in 1998 when both parts of the island voted to accept the Belfast Agreement. The sense of failure and inferiority had been banished, we thought, for good.[25]

"We are, after all, no great prize for any would-be overlord now." Who would even dignify us by having us as a colony, the *Irish Times* weeps? Failure and inferiority are the lot of the Irish, the editorial argues. If only "we" could be a colony again, to restore our own confidence in ourselves. But this "we," which looks more collectivizing than it really is, did not make decisions through market signals, but in board rooms. The "we" is being given traits and a coherent collective agency which it doesn't have. Indeed, an essentializing discourse with regard to "Irishness" has been a repeated reaction to the financial crisis. In the aforementioned documentary "People & Power — Collapse of the Celtic Tiger," the voice-over emphasizes that Ireland tends to bow down to particular social groups — priests and bankers are offered as examples — as if to delineate the physiognomy of a race. Anne Mulhall's article "Mind Yourself" and Conor McCabe's *The Sins of the Father* take aim at this particular reaction to the crisis. Mulhall's article builds on Lauren Berlant's analysis of neoliberalism's cruel optimism, which she defines as a continued attachment to a form of life that no longer makes sense, and demonstrates how Maureen Gaffney, a popular media personality, promulgates this cruel optimism for the Irish

---

25 "Was It for This?" *The Irish Times*, November 28, 2010.

public.²⁶ Well-being and resilience are ideal to forming neoliberal subjects, especially in the context of global deindustrialization. As peripheral EU states were restructured, Ireland proudly wore its quantitative happiness for all to see.²⁷ Mulhall shows that there is an essentializing ethnic and racial discourse underpinning statements by prominent media personalities such as Maureen Gaffney, inculcating in the viewing public absurd and unscientific notions about intrinsic properties of happiness and resilience in "Irish" people. Mulhall contextualizes this with research on suicide and self-harm, giving the lie to the assumption that the "Irish" are resilient. Conor McCabe, meanwhile, has analyzed the discourse around the "Irish property gene," an idea that the intergenerational trauma of losing land to the English meant that the Irish phenotype was particularly susceptible to the vagaries of property bubbles.²⁸ The Irish state has a subtle mono-ethnic basis — in particular, the "Celts" — despite successive invasions and integrations. The *Irish Times* editorial above, like many reactions to the crisis, draws a charmed circle with the crude instrument of the chummy pronoun "we," sneaking various racial, gendered, and class-based assumptions in under its penumbra. We will see this issue arise in the poetry of Leontia Flynn and we have already seen in complex acts of interpellation and omission in Joyce's "Capital Accounts."

In opposition, both Fine Gael (a liberal-conservative and Christian-democratic political party) and the Labour Party could complain about the promissory note, or bank guarantee, given to banks in 2008. Two years later, because of the promissory note, the IMF had to give the Irish state a loan. After the 2011 general election, Fine Gael and the Labour Party formed a coalition government, and did not alter anything. With the so-called Prom Night Bill of 2013, the Irish government shuf-

---

26 See Lauren Berlant, *Cruel Optimism* (Durham: Duke University Press, 2011).
27 Anne Mulhall, "Mind Yourself: Well-being and Resilience as Governmentality in Contemporary Ireland," *The Irish Review* 53 (2017), 29–44, at 35.
28 Conor McCabe, *The Sins of the Father: The Decisions That Ahaped the Irish Economy* (Dublin: The History Press, 2013), 57–59.

fled some papers and then concluded that the problem of the promissory note and its legality had been fixed. They rushed a bill through the Dáil, jetting President Michael D. Higgins from Italy to sign it into effect as soon as possible; it was alleged that this was because of a "leak" to foreign media. On TV3, Ursula Halligan said that the "leak came from Frankfurt's end." It later emerged that Frankfurt had not been consulted, and the leak was probably non-existent. On the night of February 6, 2013, the Irish Bank Resolution Corporation (IBRC) was liquidated after the Fine Gael/Labour coalition passed emergency overnight legislation through the Oireachtas. The IBRC was the name given to the entity formed in 2011 by the court-mandated merger of the state-owned banking institutions Anglo Irish Bank and Irish Nationwide Building Society. This was the night before the Irish Supreme Court was due to hear an appeal by David Hall, a Dublin businessman. He was challenging the legality of the bank guarantee. Hall's argument before the High Court was that the payment of the €31 billion in promissory notes in respect of the now defunct Anglo Irish Bank was illegal as it was not approved by a Dáil vote. The High Court ruled that he did not have the locus standi to challenge the legality of the €3.06 billion promissory note payment that was due at the end of March. As Conor McCabe points out, the Prom Night Bill retrofitted legality onto the actions of the Dáil when it offered the bank guarantee. McCabe refers to this legislation as an exercise in "creative accounting."[29] I think he is right to label it as such. But I also think there are other examples of creative accounting, under which I would include Trevor Joyce's "Capital Accounts" and Leontia Flynn's *Profit and Loss*. My point is not that their poetry is some kind of poetic correlate to the 2013 bill, but that accounting practices are incredibly creative in Ireland and that equally creative writing in Ireland heavily leans toward accounting.

---

29 Ibid., 230.

3

In a 2011 essay titled "What Do I Know? (Or, Why I Need to Give Up Post-modernism and Live an Irony-free Life)," Leontia Flynn describes her encounter with the work of fellow Northern Irish poets such as Paul Muldoon and Medbh McGuckian, whose work is described by Flynn as ironic, referential, ludic, and suspicious of authenticity. She explains why she wants avoid to emulating it stylistically:

> I want to stop clicking, scrolling and speed-reading and shuffling on to the next song, and instead focus on poetry which stays still and feels something. And this is what I want to write too. Not unmediated self-expression, of course, but not preemptively cut off with a glib reflex.[1]

My focus here is not on Flynn's assessment of what she calls postmodernism but on testing her stated intentions against her own poem "Letter to Friends," also published in 2011. Does this poem avoid glibness, that is, speaking or spoken in a confident way without careful thought? The poem has been hailed by

---

1 Leontia Flynn, "What Do I Know? (Or, Why I Need to Give Up Post-modernism and Live an Irony-free Life)," *Edinburgh Review* (2011), https://edinburgh-review.com/extracts/article-leontia-flynn/.

many as a triumph, I suspect because of the way it chimes with reactionary trends in thought in the aftermath of the financial crisis. The poem is described as an "auditing of the poet's life and times, from the vantage point of her own motherhood and marriage" and prompts the reflection that "not everything can be quantified in the way the age demands, even as these poems take the measure of their age."[2]

The poem is contained in Flynn's third book *Profit and Loss*. Flynn's "Letter to Friends" opens and closes with the poet in a car in a traffic jam. It is raining, a typical Irish summer. The text turns, in the first section, to the past, a previous generation's worries during the millennium (the Y2K bug), and asks "what has been gained or lost" since 2000. The poet's persona thinks about technology, tries to conjure wonder at the fact that before the internet there were travel agents and landlines. It sifts through all the old junk of youth, finds a photo of the poet drunk at Marx's grave. Unavoidably autobiographical, the texts show us Flynn's thoughts on her university studies, her multiple house moves, her jobs, and P45s (P45 is a reference code for a form titled Details of employee leaving work, and the term is used as a metonym for termination of employment). In the second section the poem muses on the ways in which her friends in her youth held debates about literary merit. It sneers at her students, remarking that they punctuate their sentences with too many "likes." Flynn also tries to preempt any criticism of her attitudes by remarking that she may be attacked for being a snob; in today's society, as she sees it, only people who say things are "hunky dory" are allowed to speak.[3] Naomi Marklew notes that Flynn's early work displays "cynicism,"[4] and that is also on show in "Letter to Friends":

---

2   "Fran Brearton, "Profit and Loss by Leontia Flynn — Review," *The Guardian,* September 2, 2011, https://www.theguardian.com/books/2011/sep/02/profit-loss-leontia-flynn-review.
3   Leontia Flynn, *Profit and Loss* (London: Cape, 2011), 41.
4   Naomi Marklew, "The Future of Northern Irish Poetry: Fragility, Contingency, Value and Beauty," *English Academy Review* 31 no. 2 (2014): 64–80, at 68.

> But here, though, poetry — the Holy Grail
> so long — the language at its highest power,
> has got its marks back from the public: fail
> and fail again. The reasons for this are
> a) that it's quaint and b) that it's obscure;
> its flourishes and willed opacities
> are verbal tics The People can't forgive.
> The problem is we're not sure what it's for…
> It's out of step with our capacities
> for being literal — and lucrative
>
> like visual art in London when it "Shocks!"[5]

We can hear Beckett in the "fail / and fail again." Poetry, the poem suggests, has lost its privileged place as a marker of high culture, and this failure is linked both to its quaintness and its difficulty or obscurity. "The People" enter the poem, and they cannot forgive poetry. Suddenly, Flynn's poem joins the speaker as poet with "The People" in a single pronoun ("our capacities"), to a populist denunciation of poetry. The text states that poetry is not in step with "our" need for literal meaning (or perhaps indexicality) nor is it "lucrative," that is, money-making. This question is merely one in a long series of complaints, and the point is not to find anything out but to convey how terrible everything is. Next, Flynn also lashes out at feminist discourse, bemoaning the fact that "gender" and "sex" are being problematized: "we're not quite clear who women are."[6] This strikes me as a dog whistle for hateful remarks, implying that there is uncertainty around gender and conforming to gender roles. She also laments that people don't hear enough from men these days — it is unclear, in context, how ironic this is.[7] Flynn even begins to wildly link the rise of ecopolitics to irrational faith, in some rather irrational leaps of her own: "For 'carbon footprint' try

---
5   Flynn, *Profit and Loss*, 40.
6   Ibid., 42.
7   Ibid.

replacing 'sin.'"[8] Could this possibly fall further foul of the "glib reflex" Flynn elsewhere claims to wish to avoid? Is this poetry mocking glibness? Is it ironically performing the worst possible reactionary thinking for the sake of edginess? Is the repetition of such thinking this poem's best counter to the quaintness of poetry or its loss of illusory primacy? How do these kinds of remarks come to be acceptable in poetry, ignored by reviewers, or indeed anywhere else?

---

[8] Ibid.

3.1

During the boom there was a turn to accounting in certain Irish poems, as illustrated by Flynn's title again, which names an account just as Joyce's "Capital Accounts" does. The *Oxford English Dictionary* entry for the phrase *profit and loss* notes that it comes from accounting and bookkeeping, and primarily refers to the "profit and loss account," or "the net gain and loss made in a commercial transaction or series of transactions," or "an arithmetical rule by which the gains or losses on commercial transactions are calculated." Reviewers have noted that Flynn's title is lifted from T.S. Eliot's *The Waste Land,* published in 1922, and in particular section IV, "Death by Water," in which "Phlebas the Phoenican" has died by drowning and so forgotten "the profit and the loss."[1] But Eliot's text offers us a rather bland observation: profits and losses will be forgotten when we die, living is important and the precondition of monetary concerns. Going back further in literary history, the phrase *profit and loss* typically denotes veniality and in particular anxieties about class. For example, one of its earliest uses is in Thomas Hardy's *Tess of D'Urbervilles,* published in 1891, where Mrs. Brooks is described by the narrator as follows: "She was too deeply material-

---

[1] T.S. Eliot, *The Waste Land*, in *Collected Poems 1909–1962* (London: Faber, 2002), 52–76, at 65.

ized, poor woman, by her long and enforced bondage to that arithmetical demon Profit-and-Loss, to retain much curiosity for its own sake."[2] Here, paying attention to money entails a loss of intellectual curiosity. And in Jane Austen's *Emma,* published in 1815, Emma says of Mr. Martin that in the future he "will be a completely gross, vulgar farmer — totally inattentive to appearances, and thinking of nothing but profit and loss."[3] The farmer will not come off well, he will not care about *appearances* but *money* and other pragmatic things. Thus, the phrase originates in a need to denigrate the petite bourgeoisie from the perspective of a *haute bourgeoisie.* The petty or petite bourgeoisie are a class of semi-autonomous peasantry and small merchants whose political stance often reflects or imitates the high bourgeoisie, small-scale capitalists who often work alongside their laborers. As a liminal class stratum who feel threatened from below but excluded from above, they are prone to turn their ire on scapegoated immigrants, those who do not fit the definition of a fantastical community of national belonging. Insofar as the phrase *profit and loss* is frequently used to describe a petty-bourgeois mindset, I want to suggest that Flynn's title is better served by thinking about Austen's *Emma* rather than Eliot's *Waste Land.*

Sometimes Flynn's "Letter to Friends" silently quotes Auden and Eliot — but the main touchstone for the poem is Auden's "Letter to Lord Byron," published in 1937. In *The Matter of Capital,* Nealon argues that there are "two poetic emphases" that "form the parameters of 'the matter of capital'" in twentieth-century American poetry. These derive from, on the one hand, the modernist poetics of Pound and "the importance of poetry as a stabilizing editorial arrangement," and on the other, Auden's notion of "poetry as the medium for registering obliterable life."[4] Trevor Joyce is a Poundian poet. But what, for Flynn, is obliterable life? What life makes it into her poem and what is periph-

---

2 Thomas Hardy, *Tess of D'Urbervilles* (London: Penguin, 2003 [1891]), 379.
3 Jane Austen, *Emma* (Middlesex: Penguin, 1968 [1816]), 62.
4 Chrisopher Nealon, *The Matter of Capital: Poetry and Crisis in the American Century* (Cambridge: Harvard University Press, 2011), 31.

eral? I want to come back to this question after looking at the overlays between Auden's poem and Flynn's.

Critics have remarked that "Letter to Friends" takes its form from Auden's "Letter to Lord Byron," despite the fact that Auden writes in *rhyme royale* (*abaccdd* in iambic pentameter), and Flynn composes in stanzas of ten lines with the rhyme-scheme *ababcdecde*. Auden and Louise MacNiece published *Letters from Iceland* in 1937, which contained "Letter to Byron." The book is a mix of poetry, logbook, correspondence, quotation, travel guide, and collage. Flynn notes in the first stanza of the third section of "Letter to Friends" that Auden and MacNiece couldn't have predicted that Iceland would be a "key" part in "all this mess" — that is, the mess of the financial crisis.[5] Flynn's impulse to rebut this idea implies that the thought occurred to her that Auden and MacNiece *should* have foreseen the financial crisis. But it also assumes that Iceland's role in the global financial crisis was "key." The Icelandic financial crisis involved the default of all three of the country's major privately-owned commercial banks in late 2008, because those banks were unable to refinance the privately-funded banks' short-term debt and because of a run on deposits in the Netherlands and the United Kingdom. Iceland's systemic banking collapse was the largest experienced by any country in economic history relative to the size of its economy.[6] Iceland's crisis led to a severe economic depression from 2008 to 2010 and with it, significant political unrest. The idea that Iceland played a key part is demonstrably false. However, comparisons between Ireland (in particular the Republic) and Iceland were common during the crisis, neatly summarized in the following anecdote by a trade unionist: "'I'm sure you've

---

5 Leontia Flynn, *Profit and Loss* (London: Cape, 2011), 43.
6 Matt O'Brien, "The Miraculous Story of Iceland," *The Washington Post*, June 17, 2015, https://www.washingtonpost.com/news/wonk/wp/2015/06/17/the-miraculous-story-of-iceland/; Kimberly Amadeo, "Iceland's Economy, Its Bankruptcy, and the Financial Crisis: How a Volcanic Eruption Helped Iceland Recover," *the balance*, May 30, 2019, https://www.thebalance.com/iceland-financial-crisis-bankruptcy-and-economy-3306347.

all heard the joke: what's the difference between Iceland and Ireland? One letter and six months. Well, here's the real difference: they brought down the government and we didn't."[7]

I'd like to go back to Auden's interest in Iceland, because I think that Flynn's namecheck of Iceland is ultimately because of Auden's interest. Flynn's choice of precursor implies that we should read this poem in light of Auden's comments. In his lecture "The World of the Sagas" delivered at University of Kent in October 1967, Auden states that people have both a desire to know about the primary or real world, and a desire to build secondary worlds, of myth, story, fiction — a kind of playpen or act of wish-fulfillment. Auden takes these terms from J.R.R. Tolkien, and he dubs the first the impulse of the "Historian," the second the "Poet."[8] It is Auden's view that only since industrialized society have the historian and poet impulses been divorced.[9] The divorced historian is left with mere statistics, the divorced poet "can find materials for building his secondary worlds only in his private subjectivity."[10] This leads to narcissism in the poet. It is safe to say that if Auden were consulted as to his assessment of Flynn's poem, he would place it far from realism and close to narcissism. Auden notes that the medieval *Sturlunga Saga* is more like History than Poetry. He turn to the Icelandic prose sagas as examples of what he calls "Social Realism" and says that they are extraordinary for their early date and their literary merit, which for Auden surpasses the realism of nineteenth century novels.[11] He claims Iceland was a "rural democracy" very early on: because it was a small and almost classless society, realism was possible.[12] In his 1965 foreword to *Letters from Iceland,* Auden notes that Icelandic society is "still the only really

---

7   Dan Finn, "Ireland on the Turn?" *New Left Review* 67 (2011): 5–39, at 34n40.
8   W.H. Auden, *Secondary Worlds* (London: Faber, 1968), 41.
9   Ibid., 73.
10 Ibid., 74.
11 Ibid., 48, 51. Auden says that the objectivity of the sagas is "astounding" at 65.
12 Ibid., 54, 55.

classless society I have ever encountered."[13] For Auden, Iceland is a kind of political fantasy—where historian and poet are reunited, where there are *no classes*. It was also somewhere he went during the rise of fascism in Europe for respite.

All of these interests have a role in Auden's "Letter to Lord Byron," because the poem is a meditation on what has happened to art since the Industrial Revolution, written with an eye on the aftermath of a Wall Street Crash and the rise of fascism. In Section I, Auden states that "novel writing is / A higher art than poetry altogether / In my opinion, and success implies / Both finer character and faculties."[14] It is now, he tells Byron, "the most prodigious of the forms."[15] And a touchstone of the novel's rise, in Auden's view, is Jane Austen. Addressing Byron, Auden writes that "You could not shock her more than she [Austen] shocks me" and that James Joyce is "innocent as grass" compared to her, because she reveals the "economic basis of society."[16] Austen is more offensive and shocking to Auden than Byron, because she explores the relationship between love and money. The economic basis of society weighs heavily on Auden's mind because of the Great Depression of 1927, just as it weighs on Flynn's in the aftermath of the crisis of 2007–8.

Auden characterizes John Bull, symbol of England and the English, as a "secretary" to the "ogre" of fascism:

> He dreads the ogre, but he dreads yet more
>   Those who conceivably might set him free,
> Those the cartoonist has no time to draw.
>   Without his bondage he'd be all at sea;
>   The ogre need but shout "Security,"

---

13 W.H. Auden and Louise MacNeice, *Letters from Iceland* (London: Faber, 1985), 10.
14 W.H. Auden, *Collected Longer Poems* (London: Faber, 2012), 40.
15 Ibid., 40.
16 Ibid., 41.

To make this man, so lovable, so mild,
As madly cruel as a frightened child.[17]

In times of difficulty, and especially after the Great Depression, fascism (now as a dragon) rises:

When a man sees the future without hope,
  Whenever he endorses Hobbes' report
  "The life of man is nasty, brutish, short,"
The dragon rises from his garden border
And promises to set up law and order.[18]

This, then, is how fascism arises, for Auden — people endorse Hobbes's theory that life is competitive (or "nasty" and "brutish") and begin to only care for what lies within their garden wall, and from that garden wall the dragon of fascism arises. Echoing Jordan B. Peterson's injunction to get your house in order, people are encouraged to not think beyond their private property or private sphere — their "garden." Byron, who the poem is addressed to, is the polar opposite:

You never were an Isolationist;
  Injustice you had always hatred for,
And we can hardly blame you, if you missed
  Injustice just outside your lordship's door:
  Nearer than Greece were cotton and the poor.
Today you might have seen them, might indeed
Have walked in the United Front with Gide,[19]

There is some weird anacoluthon, or syntactical reversal, in the second line there to make the rhyme work, and we will see a more suspect example of rhyme enforcements in Flynn's poem. The poem praises Byron for not being small-minded but criti-

---

17 Ibid., 53.
18 Ibid., 55.
19 Ibid., 54.

cizes him for spotting injustice in Greece before he saw injustice at home in the form of poverty. Auden notes that today Byron would have noticed poverty at home and abroad and joined the United Front. Though for Auden it may have been better to start with charity at home and poverty in Britain, he is also clearly sympathetic to Byron's leanings. The United Front referenced here is probably a nod towards the USSR's 1935 International Writers' Congress, at which Gide was present to pledge assistance in the struggle against fascism.[20]

Like Keatinge and O'Driscoll, Flynn's poem mainly takes aim at consumerism. Her critique of consumerism runs as follows:

> Belfast aspires to be, then, every place
> where shopping is done less for recreation
> (this might apply to all the western race)
> than from a kind of civic obligation.[21]

But here we have, unproblematized, the notion of a "western race." And if one were to offer the excuse that it is simply there to fulfil a rhyme scheme, it would simply further indict the glibness of the poem in both form and content. Flynn's poem does not think beyond its garden border, the apparently self-contained form of its rhyme scheme. From Flynn's rhyme scheme, if you look closely, you can see a dragon rise. And it comes through forcefully in the poem's close.

---

20 Orlando Figes, *Revolutionary Russia, 1891–1991* (London: Penguin, 2014), 295–96: "Through the United Front the Soviet Union won over many sympathizers in the West. Soviet propaganda portrayed the USSR as the leader of 'progressive humanity,' as the world's only socialist state, and as its main hope against the fascist threat. Western intellectuals were taken in. In June 1935, a Moscow-financed International Writers' Congress for the Defence of Culture was held in Paris at which famous writers such as André Gide, E.M. Forster and Aldous Huxley declared their solidarity with their Soviet comrades in the struggle against fascism."
21 Flynn, *Profit and Loss*, 41.

3.2

The economy of the Republic was much weaker than that of the North throughout the twentieth century, due to its agricultural basis on small farms. Protectionism was introduced by Seán Lemass in 1932, and the economy became isolated. From 1945 to 1960 Ireland missed out on the European economic boom across Europe, and emigration remained high. Meanwhile, the North's industry, based on shipbuilding, ropes, shirts and textiles, declined from 1960, and then more so due to the "Troubles." The Northern Irish government has run a deficit for many years, and is completely dependent on an annual subvention from London. "Letter to Friends" describes all of the changes that Belfast has undergone, especially since the Good Friday Agreement in 1994.

Having pointed out some of the more troubling aspects of Flynn's work, I'd like to discuss how and where economics pops up in this poem. The first stanza of the third section of "Letter to Friends" opens with a comment on the emotional impact of the news that "several banks" have collapsed.[1] In the fourth line of it we get the rather clumsy repetition of "ripple" in "ripples on a ripple tank." Then we get plays with other forms of water or

---

1 Leonita Flynn, *Profit and Loss* (London: Cape, 2011), 43.

liquid, "frozen," turns into "liquidity" in the financial sense, that is, the interchangeability of assets and money.

The second stanza of the third section contains three sets of brackets conveying a sense of extraneous verbiage and doubt. The first is "(it seems)."[2] We are given the basic narrative that house prices rose and men in suits sold *future* prices to poorer people. Nobody is named here; all is a mass of confusion undercut by the bracketed *it seems*. Then we are given an etymology of mortgage, undercut again by an *apparently*. This poetry is anecdotal and provides information prosaically, and that information is often delivered with a significant caveat. While this may reflect the reality that the economy is *far away*, it feels abstract and distant and increasingly appears to be governed by extremely obscure technical equations and densely packed networks of debt and credit, whether moral and fiscal. It also allows for suspect movements in the poem. While we should seemingly be unsure of what the economy is, lacking certainty about gender is also a problem for the poem. But right after that "it seems", the poet quickly zips through a series of metaphors: a bubble, cash as wetness that is dried up *by* the bubble, which has transformed into a cloth, and then a ship filled with credit and cash sinking, presumably surrounded by water again and thereby more potential cash.

In the third stanza of the third section Flynn mentions her trip to "sunny Bergen." It is the second holiday mentioned in three stanzas.[3] Almost half of this stanza consists of a bracketed book review of Cormac MacCarthy's *The Road*, published in 2006. In *The Road* a father and his young son journey across post-apocalyptic America some years after an extinction event. The emotions elicited by the financial crisis have been doubt and fear so far, but we have a very intense burst of hatred here, and a violent description of suicide. The most intense emotional reaction the poem musters is in response to a book. *The Road* evinces repugnance because the speaker is upset about its post-

---

2   Ibid.
3   Ibid., 44.

apocalyptic setting and its nihilism. But *The Road* is also quite conservative in its desire to establish some remnant of a nuclear family and preserve the child as a sacred figure of futurity. The speaker is a mother, as the fifth stanza makes clear when it mentions the "grinding week-long days" of "new motherhood."[4] The fourth stanza moves to Flynn's father, who suffers from Alzheimer's: "The heart that breaks / daily at each new symptom of decline / isn't my own (abstraction I can bear…) / and then that bubble bursts."[5] Here, the second stanza's bursting bubble, evoking the housing bubble, becomes personal feeling, a feeling of heartbreak. A bubble bursts and the sadness of living with her father's disease overwhelms her. Flynn moves our attention back to lived experience. Flynn's poem moves, I think, away from money and debt. It goes towards obligation, in particular the obligation a mother has to her child and in turn the obligation of the child to the mother. The relationship between a mother and child is, much more clearly than most relationships, widely held to be incommensurable, and defining something as incommensurate is a "special form of valuing. Incommensurables preclude trade-offs."[6] Although markets structure the entire basis of the family's relations, Flynn retreats into the family, or at least her ability to have a child or not, staying within this garden wall. The ostensible sanctity of the family offers some momentary shelter, but at quite a cost.

This is the final stanza:

A dove, an olive branch, a ray of light.
Who would have thought that only for so long
might downturns turn down; that the future's bright
and *black*? That one new Power's age-old wrong
should find redress, or symbol of redress
— and underneath her blanket with its bear

---

4   Ibid.
5   Ibid.
6   Wendy Nelson Espeland and Mitchell L. Stevens, "Commensuration as a Social Process," *Annual Review of Sociology* 24 (1998): 313–43, at 326.

my baby daughter too now lies at ease;
she's six months old. The future's all a guess.
My heap of junk is ready for the fire;
our lives stand waiting, primed for compromise.[7]

What does Flynn mean when she writes "the future's bright / and *black*?" Why does Flynn italicize this word? She seems surprised that the future has this color — that the future is colored, and that the future is a thing that can be both bright and the darkest of hues, that something can be bright and yet devoid of light. It is obviously racist, and this kind of racism is perfectly palatable for many readers of poetry — that's why so many reviewers can read it untroubled and laud it. Remember the complaints about free speech (one can only say certain things, i.e., that things are "hunky dory") and the implicit offense at the fact that some people have lost certainty about what "women" are. I would like to set these lines against Fred Moten's essay "The Subprime and the Beautiful," which "assumes an irreducible relation between preservation and celebration and considers the subprime crisis to be a moment that requires and also allows practitioners of black studies to develop ways of integrating celebration and critique."[8] Because Flynn's poem seems so troubled by blackness, I want to quote Moten at length on the financial crisis and blackness:

> Consider the subprime debtor as guerilla, establishing pockets of insurgent refuge and marronage, carrying revaluation and disruptively familial extensions into supposedly sanitized zones. Deployed by the imposition of severalty, demobilized from the general project, she infiltrates domesticity, restages race war's theater of operations under the anarchic principles of poor theater. In this, she extends and remodels the freedom movement's strategies of nonexclusion, where

---

7   Flynn, *Profit and Loss,* 45.
8   Fred Moten, "The Subprime and the Beautiful," *African Identities* 11, no. 2 (2013): 237–45, at 237.

> courts of law were turned into jurisgenerative battlefields, where public schools and public accommodations became black study halls, greyhounds-contra-hellhounds, where fugitive spirits, sometimes misconstrued as evil or void even by themselves, take freedom rides on occasions that parallel the radical commensality of the counter-lunch. The subprime debtor, in the black radical tradition of making a way out of no way (out), is also a freedom fighter, a community disorganizer, a suburban planner.[9]

While Moten celebrates the black people moving to white neighborhoods on credit as freedom-fighters, Flynn's poem disengages from black life, expressing violently polite and oblique shock that the future might be colored, or more specifically, not solely *white,* and thereby exhibits fear of a *black* future. From its garden wall rises the specter of a "western race"-based capitalism as a new means of rallying and closing of the ranks in a shuffle towards, if not profitability, then exclusion.

Flynn's poem is *messed up.* But here it is, published by a major poetry publisher, sold in bookshops, and lauded in newspapers. Joyce's poem indexes the ways in which the metaphors it draws on miss things out or don't completely map onto each other or force us to think carefully. Joyce's poem, I think, foregrounds the inadequacy of the transpositions it engages in, but Flynn's poem ends up being a reactionary flailing against an abstracted Blackness, as well as individuals who are gender nonconforming, and indeed anyone who believes in global warming. I have pointed out some repugnant features in this poem, and, while this does not exonerate the poet or poem, the poem *is* self-aware in this regard and asks explicitly for forgiveness: "Forgive me."[10] But the whole poem, including this abject plea, is in bad faith.

---

9 Ibid., 243.
10 Flynn, *Profit and Loss,* 43.

4

On May 20, 2009 the report on the Commission to inquire into child abuse, also known as the Ryan Commission, offered a devastating insight into the scale of abuse of children in Ireland from 1936 onwards. It was followed a few months later by the Murphy Report. It was a strange time, and I remember acutely the upset around me and the prevalence of debate in the media about the abuse scandals in pubs and workplaces. Four years later Enda Kenny apologizes to victims of the Magdalene Laundries, saying the government and citizens of Ireland "deeply regret and apologise unreservedly to all those women for the hurt that was done to them."[1] (The Magdalene Laundries in Ireland were institutions usually run by Roman Catholic orders, which operated from the eighteenth to the late twentieth centuries, ostensibly to house "fallen women." They and their children were typically buried in unmarked mass graves on the grounds, which continue to be

---

[1] Miriam Lord, "'I, as Taoiseach, on behalf of the State, the Government and our citizens, deeply regret and apologise unreservedly to all those women for the hurt that was done to them'," *The Irish Times*, February 20, 2013, https://www.irishtimes.com/news/i-as-taoiseach-on-behalf-of-the-state-the-government-and-our-citizens-deeply-regret-and-apologise-unreservedly-to-all-those-women-for-the-hurt-that-was-done-to-them-1.1313278.

uncovered.)[2] The scandal is merely another in a litany. In 2014, a year after Kenny's apology, an essay came out in an academic publication which was unreservedly on the side of the Church. In it, Brendan Geary points out that the Irish state and Catholic morality are yoked together in the Irish habitus.[3] Geary gives a narrative of the financial crisis in Ireland which sets it side-by-side with the "agonies" of the Church, punished both by secularism's cruel tendencies, revelations about the sexual abuse of children, and the long-known Magdalene Laundries. For Geary, the revelations prompted critical reflections in formerly passive participants (i.e., the wider community), and in turn Irish people apparently turned to the Celtic Tiger for solace, having been hidden under a rock on the Blasket Isles beforehand. And yet, relishes Geary, this Celtic Tiger would also turn out to "have feet of clay."[4] Geary implies that being a child-rape-apologist is defendable. Is Cardinal Brady, Geary pines, not "by all accounts a good, compassionate, pastoral man"? Can we not forget that all he did was neglect to inform parents or secular authorities of the abuse of children? Is this, he asks us in a tone of disbelief, all it takes to drag a *perfectly reasonable* man through the dirt?[5] Out of the frying pan, into the fire, apparently. Geary's argument moves dizzyingly between the moral reprobation of situations in which the economy and abuse of individuals seem distant, such as under capitalism, and closer, as in the observation that Irish Catholics must have "colluded" with this abuse in smaller communities. This is simultaneously absurd and unavoidable.

---

2 Jamie Grierson, "Mass Grave of Babies and Children Found at Tuam Care Home in Ireland," *The Guardian,* March 3, 2017, https://www.theguardian.com/world/2017/mar/03/mass-grave-of-babies-and-children-found-at-tuam-orphanage-in-ireland; Carol Ryan, "Irish Church's Forgotten Victims Take Case to U.N.," *The New York Times,* May 25, 2011, https://www.nytimes.com/2011/05/25/world/europe/25iht-abuse25.html.
3 Brendan Geary, "Shattered Assumptions: A Tale of Two Traumas," in *From Prosperity to Austerity: A Socio-Cultural Critique of the Celtic Tiger and Its Aftermath* (Manchester: Manchester University Press, 2014), 47–61, at 47, 49.
4 Ibid., 50.
5 Ibid., 57.

It is absurd because we know that although our lives are predicated on the suffering and exclusion of others, we feel it to be the case that this suffering is frequently at such a distance that we cannot do anything to counteract it. Geary is a Marist Brother (a monk, a member of an international community of Catholic Religious Institute of Brothers) and hence much more complicit than you or I in the systematic rape of children, and in writing this defense of the Church, is certainly an apologist-*cum*-colluder-extraordinaire to said rape. Geary's claim that many people colluded in this abuse is of course true, but the jumps between this and his observations about the Celtic Tiger as some kind of collective moral failing prompt confusion. In what sense are any of these distinct categories, that is, sexual abuse and economic power, relatable? The position that Geary occupies assumes the economy to have a moral basis. If we retreat from that assumption, we will wonder on what order we can appeal for justice, both from the failures of capitalism and the Church to offer a just life. These same dizzying switches in Geary's account, which are indefensible, unavoidable, and upsetting, are evoked to a lesser degree by the work of Dave Lordan that compares the financial crisis to situations of sexualized violence.

A multi-genre writer, performer, editor, and educator, Dave Lordan has taught creative writing across Ireland. His poem "A resurrection in Charlesland" figures the Celtic Tiger and subsequent economic crash as sexual abuse. Charlesland is a high-density development located on the southside of Greystones in County Wicklow, Ireland, about twenty-five kilometers from Dublin city center. Charlesland has about 1,500 houses and apartments and a neighborhood shopping complex with a supermarket. The poem has twenty-one sections demarcated by currency symbols that cut across the poem. The first break is signaled by six dollar signs, the next seven pound signs, the next six euros, then seven dollars, then six euros again, then dollars, pounds, pounds, dollars, euros, dollars, pounds, euros, six Xs, dollars, pounds, euros, pounds, dollars, then euros, striating the poem's continuous emission. It may be that Lordan is saying that these currencies simultaneously unite and divide the poem.

These currencies are surely the loudest language we now have, the only language we speak to each other. Speaking to this point, in the essay "A History of Separation," the Endnotes collective claims that "the communist horizon of the present" is not "class consciousness" but rather

> a growing consciousness of capital. At present, workers name the enemy they face in different ways: as bad banks and corrupt politicians, as the greedy 1%. These are, however, only foreshortened critiques of an immense and terrible reality. Ours is a society of strangers, engaged in a complex set of interactions. There is no one, no group or class, who controls these interactions. Instead, our blind dance is coordinated impersonally, through markets. The language we speak — by means of which we call out to one another, in this darkness — is the language of prices. It is not the only language we can hear, but it is the loudest. This is the community of capital.[6]

While Lordan and Joyce decry fat cats or estate agents, they are very conscious of prices and currencies, as is clear in the currency symbols of "A resurrection in Charlesland" and the Foreign Domestic Investment of Joyce's "Capital Accounts."

Lordan's poem is free verse and clearly exhibits the influence of the Surrealists and the Beats. "A resurrection in Charlesland" describes a state of affairs in which the media has turned against the public, putting it under a "siege," and also mentions "a brutal commentariat" ("all the high-toned Pinochets / on the Radio") calling for "slashing" of the public sector via cuts to funding.[7] Under the influence of the free-market-oriented neoliberal Chicago Boys, the military government of Pinochet implemented economic liberalization including currency stabilization, re-

---

[6] "A History of Separation: The Defeat of the Workers' Movement," *Endnotes* 4 (2015): 70–192, at 166, https://endnotes.org.uk/issues/4/en/endnotes-the-defeat-of-the-workers-movement.

[7] Lordan, *Invitation to a Sacrifice* (Clare: Salmon, 2010), 108.

moval of tariff protections for local industry (as in Whitaker's plan), and the banning of trade unions, privatized social security, and hundreds of state-owned enterprises. These policies produced what has been referred to by right-wing libertarian Milton Friedman as the "Miracle of Chile," which was, for most of the 1990s, the best performing economy in Latin America. In Lordan's poem, one of those "Pincohets" is almost certainly the "Friedmanite" Colm McCarthy from University College Dublin, who appeared regularly on Irish Radio during the composition of this poem.[8] The "Nation" is "For Sale" and although the populace repeat the "neoliberal prescriptions" they are offered — people were swindled out of money for houses, but also enjoyed being swindled. Drugs and entrepreneurship are intertwined as the poem discusses various forms of abuse and "solicitors" with penchants for stimulants, punning on "Charlie" as cocaine and Charlie McGreevy, minister for Finance during the Celtic Tiger years.[9] It offers Bertie Ahern, Tony Blair, and the "mid-fall USA" as the cause of the crisis.[10] The poem describes the lead-up to the financial crisis like this:

> Estate agents casinoed our existences
> spun a wheel with only one bright number on it,
> Looking-After-Number 1
>   kept plying the line that everyone
>   was guaranteed to be a millionaire,
>   for starters,
>
>   till we were hot-cheeked with money lust
> and then they swayed their magic keys in front of us
> like hypnorapists goofing us
> for all possible advantage.
>
> Bankers brought the kinky costumes and equipment.

---

8 Ibid.
9 Ibid., 114.
10 Ibid., 116.

> Adpimps supplied the glitterdust and lube.
> Channel 4 filmed every oiled up inch and second of it
> flatscreening it back to us
> as we squatted
>
> on the chaise-longue for years
> to watch ourselves being screwed
> while being screwed
> on the chaise longue for years…
>
>> and most of us knew what was happening
>> and some of us truly were hoodwinked
>> and nearly everybody wanted it never to stop.
>
> Thus were we rightly sodomed here and dumped
> two million life-indentured gimps
> stuck without an exit plan
> in one of time's bogged-down pauses,
> history's less-interesting amber phases […][11]

Lordan's poetic voice here rails against an immorality — "casino" is made into a verb to describe what estate agents have done, and selfishness, sexual passion, and "money-lust" are joined together. The public are "screwed" on a chaise longue by these estate agents, who are assisted by bankers and "Adpimps." The "amber phases" are the moment on a traffic light where you pause to give way to others. In the twelfth section a character named "MBA Tina," and of course TINA is the acronym for the neoliberal slogan daily chanted by politicians, "There Is No Alternative," holds a Masters in Business Administration. This character watches porn, no doubt the porn made by the estate agents. The fact that the poem claims "we" were "sodomed" and then "dumped" implies that those doing this are murderous rapists.

Another of Lordan's poems which describes sexual abuse is "Nightmare Pastoral." The poem is incredibly prosaic; it deliv-

---

11   Ibid., 110–11.

ers information clearly. The poem introduces something that is "too absurd" to be considered a "rumour," and so the poem designates it a "lie." The lie is that Chilean Roberto Bolaño visited a village in the "west of ireland" in 1969. On July 20, 1969 the Eagle landed on the Moon as part of the Apollo 11 mission, and three months later on November 19, 1969 the Intrepid on the Apollo 12 mission landed. Bolaño was journeying from a riot in Mexico to one in Paris. The poet pretends to have access to Bolaño's diaries and mentions how Bolaño writes about his time in Ireland. Bolaño is in a pub in a village on the day of the moon landing, and he gets very drunk. That night, in a dream, "two pissed priests are raping / a nine year old girl / up a boreen (he says 'grassy lane')." The brackets posture the diary as primary source. The content is shocking and the language banal, the unimportant brackets coming in again in a manner reminiscent of Flynn's poem, to put us slightly off kilter. The priests then "strangle and dump / her out the back door" of the van. Two guards in the dream investigate the crime and are about to arrest the priests, when they "are told / in no uncertain terms / by the powers that be / to close the case / and forget all about it." A bishop orders the priests to go and convert people in "remotest Africa." Bolaño describes the nightmare the next day to his fellow drinkers in the village pub, and they claim that Bolaño must have had a bad pint. Bolaño gets "very, very drunk" and is arrested "for his own safety / and to preserve public order." The poem ends: "This is the kind of thing / he would later go on / to write about."[12] The poet-activist Sarah Clancy has a similar poem, noting that Bolaño "stole" her "best lines / and binned them / before I'd invented them."[13] Binning, dumping, extraneous refuse.

Why do these poets feel so close to Bolaño? One way to answer this would be to think about what this poet-novelist later went on to write. *2666* is the last novel by Roberto Bolaño. It was released in 2004, a year after Bolaño's death. It revolves around

---

12 Ibid., 43–45.
13 Sarah Clancy, *Truth & Other Stories* (Clare: Salmon, 2011), 77.

an elusive German author and the unsolved and ongoing murders of women in Santa Teresa, a violent city inspired by Ciudad Juárez in Mexico and its epidemic of female homicides. "The Part about the Crimes" in Bolaño's *2666* chronicles the murders of 112 women in Santa Teresa from 1993 to 1997. In the real Ciudad Juarez, the shockingly high murder rates of women began in 1993, one year after the signing of the North American Free Trade Agreement. This agreement led to the creation of many US-owned *maquiladoras* (manufacturing plant that imports and assembles duty-free components for export) in new Export-Processing Zones. The femicides testify to the disposability of certain forms of labor. Bolaño links neoliberalism and patriarchy with sexualized violence against subaltern women through "impassive repetition of horror," thereby showcasing a system that privileges profit over life. "The Part about the Crimes" describes the apathy of state authorities. It also highlights asymmetry by introducing the figure of a "church desecrator" who is pursued much more assiduously than the murderers of women. The novel follows the police force in their mostly fruitless attempts to solve the crimes, as well as giving clinical descriptions of the circumstances and probable causes of the various homicides. These are those who are ignored because of their worthlessness in terms of class and race in the current neoliberal arrangement.[14] The subaltern Third World is a key component to the functioning of the global economic order. Both Mexico and Ireland, as abstract and real entities, know what it is to be subservient to a nearby economic power, as well as the experience of dealing with a powerful class of priests.

What I have been trying to limn here are the ways in which different species of violence — pedophilia, rape, or other forms

---

14 Laura Barberàn Reinares, "Globalized Philomels: State Patriarchy, Transnational Capital, and the Femicides on the US–Mexican Border in Roberto Bolaño's *2666*," *South Atlantic Review* 75, no. 4 (2010): 51–72. Katherine Pantaleo has argued that, "NAFTA, as a capitalist approach, has directly created a devaluation of women and an increase in gendered violence." See "Gendered Violence: An Analysis of the Maquiladora Murders," *International Criminal Justice Review* 20, no. 4 (2010): 349–65.

of sexual violence — are pulled into discussions of the financial crisis with furious affect. We saw inklings of this in the discussion of the figures of the prostitute in Joyce's poem. In Lordan's "A resurrection in Charlesland," the Irish public ("we") take the place of the young girl in the poem "Nightmare Pastoral" and are dumped in Charlesland. But the poem resurrects them.

5

Thought-starting Clichés

Donal Ryan began writing his debut novel *The Spinning Heart* in the summer of 2010, while he was working in Limerick as a labor inspector for the National Employment Rights Authority to enforce employment rights compliance.[1] Published at the end of 2013, Ryan's novel received wide acclaim and many awards. It narrates the effects of the economic downturn as they ripple through an Irish village. Many of the village's laborers were flush with cash during the boom, but they have been left in the lurch now that the local developer and the biggest employer in the area, Pokey Burke, has skipped town. As a reviewer notes, "here, the global crisis wears the face of your neighbour."[2] This narrow focus means it is a book wherein international economic crisis is transmuted into emotional crisis, like turning a beach into nothing but sand.[3] The crisis in the novel is intimate, a neighbor

---

1 Lawrence Cleary and Donal Ryan, "How I Write," interview transcript, http://www.ulsites.ul.ie/rwc/sites/default/files/rwc_Donal_Ryan_How_I_Write%2BInterview_transcript.pdf; Gemma Kappala-Ramsamy, "Debut Author: Donal Ryan," *The Guardian,* January 13, 2013, https://www.theguardian.com/books/2013/jan/13/donal-ryan-interview-spinning-heart.
2 Justine Jordan, "The Spinning Heart by Donal Ryan — Review," *The Guardian,* November 28, 2013, https://www.theguardian.com/books/2013/nov/28/spinning-heart-donal-ryan-review.
3 Ibid. See also Emily Rapp, "'The Spinning Heart' by Donal Ryan," *Boston Globe,* March 14, 2014, https://www.bostonglobe.com/arts/2014/03/14/

rather than a stranger, and in both cases an individual rather than an impersonal set of relations. The recession has been painstakingly delimited to the local level. What I'm trying to get at is that Ryan's book has a microcosmic scope, focusing on a small village where only one property developer is to blame, Pokey Burke. Bromides from the mainstream media sneak into the text and the characters wrestle against them — as they do not have a means at their disposal to deal with or counteract this mainstream narrative. The narrative we get is a familiar one, clarioned by the mainstream media and politicians. People got greedy, there were a few bad eggs, the good times were uniformly good for every social group, and now, times are uniformly bad. If these chants were overt, they might run: What do we cut? The Public Sector. When do we cut it? Now! Those chants delivered by what Lordan calls "high-toned Pinochets" have been quantitatively mapped by Julien Mercille.[4] Although Ryan's book is emphatically not a poem, it is worth looking at it to get some context on how those chants register in literary texts.

The novel collapses into solipsism, with no interest in representing the crisis as a complex net of relations and emergent abstractions engorging themselves on living labor; it merely aims to chart the psychological impact of that crisis. We are getting a representation of a consequence, not a representation of the crisis. One reviewer notes that Ryan sketches

> the internal response to external disaster: there is a queasy, fatalistic lack of surprise among the villagers that the bubble of good fortune has burst, twisted up with 'the whole mad Irish country thing' of fearing being taken for a fool, and the bitter pleasure of being proved right by disaster.[5]

---

book-review-the-spinning-heart-donal-ryan. It is a "short, swift, brutally funny romp through the fallout of a national disaster points to the likelihood of emotional crisis when one's livelihood and purpose disappear without warning."

4   Julien Mercille, *The Political Economy and Media Coverage of the European Economic Crisis: The Case of Ireland* (London: Routledge, 2015).

5   Jordan, "The Spinning Heart by Donal Ryan — Review."

This folds into a general concern about volition, complicity, and the economy.

Ryan's book is a melodrama from start to finish, with individuals bound up inexplicably in strange exchanges, often acting in a fashion which is not in their self-interest but in the interest of a sensational plot. This is not so much for the reader but the imagined community of the village's gossiper, who the character Riain dubs the "Teacup Taliban." Each chapter has a narrator who has been affected either directly or tangentially by the collapse. It deals with ghost estates as well as infidelity, inheritance, bosses running away with money, and people emigrating to Australia. It shows how the lives of many individuals have been impacted by the recession and in particular how a middle-class uses it to squeeze lower-class employees. For example, Hillary ends up doing more work for less money, while Kate, who runs a business, is happy that, due to the recession and a climate of fear among employees, people are willing to work for less than minimum wage.[6] One reviewer bemoans that the book is "a harangue against those who powered the crazy speculation of the boom years and got away with it."[7] While Lordan's poetry displays some elements of much-needed harangue, it is absent from Ryan's novel. It is a very anxious and troubled meditation of the complicity of a small community in their own oppression by virtue of the absence of solidarity and through subtle policing of themselves and each other. This is most discernible in looking at how the text and its characters internalize and attempt to fight back against clichés. In the book Triona notes that "[p]eople say things like shouldn't we be counting our blessings that we at least have our health?"[8] Hillary muses: "Aren't you lucky to have a job? That's the stick that's used to beat us now."[9]

---

6   Donal Ryan, *The Spinning Heart* (Dublin: Doubleday Ireland, 2012), 88–89, 98.
7   Catherine Taylor, "The Spinning Heart by Donal Ryan, Review," *The Telegraph,* August 8, 2013, https://www.telegraph.co.uk/culture/books/10218878/The-Spinning-Heart-by-Donal-Ryan-review.html.
8   Ryan, *The Spinning Heart,* 153.
9   Ibid., 88.

Here, austerity is a linguistic hand-me-down. An abstracted, putatively homogenous group of people, the plain people of Ireland, say these things, or an anonymous other uses a phrase to beat someone down, to stop them from asking for more. As Triona says:

> [I]f we were all in the black we'd all be in the pink. The air is thick with platitudes around here. We'll all pull together. We're a tight-knit community. We'll all support each other. Oh really? Will we?[10]

Everything is pulverized into set phrases. Cliché is a cloak which veils, and possibly makes livable, serious problems, and those problems escalate significantly in the book. When a child is kidnapped, Bobby's wife Triona meditates on the effect the kidnapping has on the community:

> The missing child didn't put anything into perspective for anyone the way they were all saying it did, he was just tacked on to the end of the list of things that just showed you how terrible it all is and how the country is pure solid destroyed and there's no end to the heartbreak and aren't we a right show now with the television cameras and the place crawling with guards. God, I'm gone awful cross. People are scared, that's all. I know that.[11]

Riain gets angry, momentarily, and it is difficult to tell if the anger is justified or whether it has any kind of ameliorative function. She bemoans the fact that tragedies are added to a pile, an account, rather than understood on their own terms as irreducible losses. After working herself into a fury, she cancels that fury out before it has even fully begun and makes excuses for her peers. The cliché's tire the characters out in Ryan's text, even though they always return to them. Such as this:

---

10 Ibid., 154.
11 Ibid., 155.

> Every bollocks is going around cribbing about the country being fucked. It'd wear you out, so it would. The country's fucked, the country's fucked, the country's fucked; the same bollockses that were going around cribbing that the whole country was gone mad for money a few years ago. They do be below in the shops, standing in miserable circles, comparing hardships. I'd love to tell them all they're a pack of miserable wankers only they're the same pricks I'll be looking for a job off of if things pick up or London doesn't work out.[12]

Here is internal policing at its most rigorous. Characters must police themselves and comport themselves for the possibility of future employment, hedging bets in case there really are no alternatives. It is tiring to repeat the clichés that the country is fucked, and even more tiring to unpack what that cliché reveals and elides.

Because it is a melodramatic and microcosmic text, the world-historical causes of the crash are not referenced. Instead, the crash is repeatedly attributed to the very people who suffer the fall out or immoral (implicitly exceptional) characters who could have ameliorated the crash by behaving in a different manner. That attitude was and remains common, most famously it was exemplified by the remarks of Bertie Ahern, the Taoiseach who was in office from 1997 to 2008, that is, during the Celtic Tiger period. In a 2015 interview, he blamed the mishandling of the Irish economy on the plain people of Ireland, "Joe and Mary Soap," who allegedly bought second, third, and fourth homes while snorting lines of EU credit. In the aftermath of the crisis, the simple fact is that the consumerism that Bertie Ahern would lay at the door of the Soaps was never anything but their own debt peonage and a revenue stream for housing magnates, banks, hedge funds, and multinational companies.[13]

---

12 Ibid., 109–10.
13 Hugh O'Connell, "Bertie Says Crisis Caused by 'Joe Soap and Mary Soap' Getting Too Many Loans," *The Journal,* December 14, 2015, https://www.thejournal.ie/bertie-ahern-joe-and-mary-soap-2501249-Dec2015/.

Ryan's book is documenting specific lives, the lives of those impacted by the recession. The cause of the recession is a person, Pokey Burke. There is no sense, in the novel, either that a class of people or a government may have been responsible or that transnational capital may have had an impact. The novel is blinkered in that regard and this is crystallized in the character Lloyd's attitude. One might say that the novel itself is an exercise in the kind of solipsism that Lloyd subscribes to in the following quote:

> I remember when I told Trevor I'd decided to be a solipsist. He laughed like a fat, retarded duck. He *honked* at me. Wow, he said, that's like a *really* good excuse to give yourself for not having a *job*. I disgusted myself by suddenly dropping my cloak of aloof superiority and becoming defensive. I can't help the economy, I said, in a pathetic, loser voice. *Pardon,* the bastard said, with glee in his eyes, you can't help the *economy*? But didn't you *create* the fucking economy, being a solipsist?[14]

Here is an explicit self-condemnation. Lloyd, or Ryan, who knows or cares, has created all of this. He creates little homunculi and pushes them around on the page. This crystallizes the kind of thinking which is pretty prevalent in most accounts: individual people's desires for houses led to this. The builder Pokey Burke running off with some money led to this. Didn't you create the economy, with your desires and needs? And might the crash therefore be your fault? But another explanation for the crash is offered too. And the novel stops there. This is not *necessary* for the novel, there are examples of novels moving beyond such personalized accounts. The most accurate account would be one that holds all the variegated and sometimes conflicting desires of individuals and the power of government and that greater power of foreign direct investment, the neoliberal International Monetary Fund, and transnational capital in hand all at

---

14 Ryan, *The Spinning Heart*, 106.

once. How to do that? How to refrain from blaming individuals? How to deal with people as the personification of sets of relations? Many of the poems I am discussing demand to be read in light of these questions. Moving toward the world, they attempt to describe the world as it is, without concocting a fantasy or scaling it down to allegory, complete with singular bogeyman. Although Ryan's fantasy is instructive, he is probably more right than he realizes when he insists in an interview that his book isn't about the crash, and ergo not about anything at all.[15]

In Ryan's text literature is useless, it is not a weapon that can counter cliché. Rather, one character Rory rebukes himself for cliché and dribble and compares his own narrative to the "auld shite I used to write in English."[16] There is a sense in the book that literature cannot offer a way out, that from the age of twelve the "auld shite" written in English class was preparation for a job market and implicated in the whole mess of neoliberal statehood. But the book is cowed under by this and exhibits a tendency towards regression and silence.[17] If Ryan's novel is modernist, it is so in the vein of Joyce's *Dubliners,* offering another image of complete paralysis and stasis. But Ryan's derogation of literature is only justified in the narrow confines of Ryan's own creative practice.

---

15 "I don't think writers necessarily have a responsibility to address social issues, but to be clear-eyed and compassionate if they happen to do so. I don't mind being described or seen as a social commentator, but I hope it's obvious that my main interest lies in the chaos inside us all, in the terrible, beautiful humanity we're all afflicted with. Recession or no recession, the storms will rage on" (Kate Appleton, "True. Right Down to My Ghost. The Donal Ryan Interview," *Three Monkeys Online,* http://www.threemonkeysonline.com/donal-ryan-interview/). And since the current lot of humanity in Ireland is historically conditioned by the crash, and there is no transhistorical human condition, we must concede that he is right: his book isn't about anything at all.
16 Ryan, *The Spinning Heart,* 59.
17 "'Why can't I find the words?' asks Bobby, struggling to articulate his hatred for his father and his love for his wife. He has been silenced repeatedly throughout his life, and as the book ends is lost for words again, in the worst possible circumstances" (Jordan, "The Spinning Heart by Donal Ryan — Review").

The mixture of anger and resignation in Ryan's novel is also on display in Rachel Warriner's response to the crisis. Warriner is an art historian, curator, and critic who has published on contemporary feminist art. Warriner's *Eleven Days* is eleven poems, each written on one of the eleven days the IMF spent in Dublin. It was published in 2011 by RunAmok Press, a small press run by James Cummins and Rachel Warriner that would later publish Trevor Joyce. The chapbook is a response to that visit to Dublin as well as the protests that occurred and flurry of changing news articles that tried to document what was happening. The pamphlet offers a poetry of lyric protest and agency and fury, but also fatigue. I remember this time, the sense of outrage everywhere as the government revealed that the IMF was bailing out the country and was actually physically present in Ireland, going back on an earlier denial, and I think "20.11.10"'s lines "yesterday's news / discredited" refer to this.[18] But I can find no reference to this in newspaper articles right now. Ireland's status as a peripheral economy is front and center: "23.11.10" mentions "peripheral at best" and "uncomplicated / peripheries."[19] Later on this period is referred to as "our 'Weimar moment'™" in the poem.[20] The implication is that, like the Weimar Republic, Ireland will suffer economically at the hands of other Europeans and possibly fall into fascism. But the comparison is closed off by brackets and trademarked, no sooner stated than salable or buyable in the intellectual-property market. That German banks are imposing this is another example of history's tendency to rhyme. The poem mentions "krona comparisons," referencing the comparisons between the situation in Iceland and Ireland. One of the poems documents Warriner's return to Cork from a protest held in Dublin on November 27, 2010, and Trevor Joyce had organized an anti-state/anti-IMF protest in Cork city to coincide with that national protest.[21]

---

18 Rachel Warriner, *Eleven Days* (Cork: RunAmok, 2011), "20.11.10."
19 Ibid., "23.11.10," "18.11.10."
20 Ibid., "18.11.10."
21 Ibid., "28.11.10." Niamh O'Mahony and Trevor Joyce, "Finding a Language Use," *Jacket2*, February 3, 2014, https://jacket2.org/interviews/joyce-

5. THOUGHT-STARTING CLICHÉS

If Warriner's sequence has an overall tone, it is one of disappointment. It is disappointed with Irish politicians, the Irish public and, perhaps most interestingly, the protestors. It is not the kind of work which, say, Jodi Dean would decry as a mere celebration of protest as a transformative personal moment, after which everyone just goes home. Indeed, Warriner seems dissatisfied with the protest form itself. For example, the poem "26.11.10" seems to *declaim* in the lines "we stride forth / in fury exhibition," but the bombast of "stride forth" is in irreducible tension with the "fury exhibition"—the "fury" is undercut by the "exhibition," as it is fury *performed* rather than simply fury itself. The protest enters the clean, clinical, white space of a gallery opening. This sense of disappointment in protestors is also present in "27.11.10":

halfmasked drinkers
crush cans in shows of fury
and small children
riot over who
holds the sign[22]

If this section might also be read as an image of unbounded energy, the general tone of the poems seems to be one of fatigue (the final line closes off in a very final ending, "sold out and done") alongside a righteous anger which is finding it difficult to select and maintain its sights on a valid target.[23] It is a poetry of protest, but it is also one suspicious of this self-fashioning.

In Warriner's poetry the lyric seems to have a counterforce at its disposal, even as it gobbles down fragments of the everyday chorus and repurposes them, as when in "25.11.10" she writes "i'd cry for you / if the IMF hadn't seized / my tearducts."[24] Here, the surreal image paradoxically short circuits any simple attribution

---

2011-finding-language-use.
22 Warriner, *Eleven Days*, "27.11.10."
23 Ibid., "28.11.10."
24 Ibid., "25.11.10."

of emotion: the speaker of the poem cannot cry, but as readers we are aware of the seizure of those previously private tear ducts as a violence that produces this lack of emotional reaction.

This poetry drags us right into the fray and namechecks those who are, in their flesh and blood, responsible for imposing austerity or have some complicity with it as well as those who struggled against it — then-EU Commissioner Olli Rehn and the University College Cork Student Union leader Daithi Linnane — and writes under the immense pressure of a historical moment, almost in panic, out of necessity. At around this time, Linnane was organizing a march against the rise in student fees. If the telescoping of Joyce's poetry makes a weird kind of ethics possible, or draws us to an archaic or possibly problematic one, Warriner's total investment in the moment, the *now* of the poems, comes at the problem in another way as protest is critiqued for being too time-bound or inadequate as a spontaneous act or performance in a moment within a time-bound poem.

In Lordan's "A resurrection in Charlesland," Lordan names the clichés and other prescriptions given to people during the Crisis:

Force-feeding ourselves Dan Brown, valium, parox,
Gerry Ryan and angelology,

we repeat the neo-liberal prescriptions:
*staying in is the new going out
and there is no such thing as society*[25]

This is practically spat out, embittered, an implicit put-down of Dan Brown, medication, talk-show host Gerry Ryan, and quasi-mystic Christianity. Lordan notes that neoliberal phrases encourage the saving of money and quotes Margaret Thatcher's sentiment that society doesn't exist. The neoliberal prescriptions are these clichés, and in Warriner's "19.11.10," the poem quotes some more linguistic detritus in order to distance itself from

---

25 Lordan, *Invitation to a Sacrifice* (Clare: Salmon, 2010), 109.

the fatalism which certain set phrases foster: "'we had a feeling this might happen' / they say / as if that would help."[26] This is a poetry of utter contempt and scorn that must ceaselessly beat back against the onslaught of cliché. Lordan and Warriner, then, voice opposition to the cliché by claiming that it does not help to "say" the cliché, and separates it out with quotation marks, while Lordan italicizes it.

Clichés also become fodder in the poetry of Mairéad Byrne. Byrne emigrated from Ireland to the US in 1994. She has been published by presses big and small in the US and Ireland, and there is something resolutely Irish about the clichés that Byrne handles. Her book *You Have to Laugh, New + Selected Poems* was published in 2013, and on one of its pages we get three poems, each entitled "YOU NEVER KNOW" with a set of brackets after it and a word describing roughly the ways in which the cliché has been worked with. This is the poem entitled "YOU NEVER KNOW (*loose*)":

You never know.
You never really know.
You never really know now do you.
You never know.
You just never know.[27]

On the next page is the poem "ARE YOU KIDDING ME?":

Are YOU kidding me?
Are you KIDDING ME?
Are you kidding me?
Are you kidding me?
ARE you KIDDING me?
Are you *kidding* me?
Are you kidding me?

---

26 Warriner, *Eleven Days*, "19.11.10."
27 Mairéad Byrne, *You Have to Laugh, New + Selected Poems* (New York: Barrow Street Press, 2013), 7.

Are *you* kidding me?
ARE YOU KIDDING ME?[28]

Sometimes nothing changes, as between lines three and four, and other times italics or capitals are added to change emphasis, tone, or meaning. Next in the selected is the title poem "YOU HAVE TO LAUGH":

You have to laugh
You have to laugh
Ah you have to laugh
You hafta laugh
You hafta laugh though
Don't you just have to laugh
You hafta laugh
Ah you hafta laugh
You have to laugh
You have to laugh
fuckit[29]

Why have I beaten you over the head with these repetitive poems? Why has the poet? These poems simultaneously mock our collective tendency to use clichés while pointing to the multiple ways they can be changed, the little modulations which ever so slightly change their meaning. "YOU NEVER KNOW," "ARE YOU KIDDING ME?," and "YOU HAVE TO LAUGH" seem to be a sequence, and the final line of the sequence "fuckit" throws all of it under the bus. If this poetry knows it has to start from the toxic clichés circulating around it, it also knows intimately the experience of burnout, tiredness, frustration, giving up. And that seems to me to be an emblematic gesture across responses to the crisis in poetry, to mix extraordinary effort and work, as in the insistent pullulations of clichés, the attempt to give them some pliancy, or soften and manipulate them, or digest them

---

28 Ibid., 8.
29 Ibid., 9.

and spit them back into the faces of one's enemies. And then the poems give up, they feel sad they have to do this at all, they get tired of it.

6

Futures

Concerning the future as it is currently conceived, Dave Lordan's "A resurrection in Charlesland" says, "tomorrow salts the sugarloaf / tomorrow cancels poetry and physics."[1] The feeling is pervasive. In the tenth poem of Joyce's *The Immediate Future* published in 2013, futurity produces wounds:

> when every least
> circumstance
> bears already
> the wounds
> of its futurity[2]

Futurity, for Lordan and Joyce, is damaging. These lines echo popular sentiments and concerns explored in a myriad number of ways by many, including not only those protesters who chanted "No Future" at anti-austerity protests around the world but also economists who were forced to reconsider whether infinite economic growth is possible let alone desirable. Tomor-

---

1   Lordan, *Invitation to a Sacrifice* (Clare: Salmon, 2010), 124.
2   Trevor Joyce, *The Immediate Future* (Cork: RunAmok, 2013), at 14. An earlier draft appeared online as "Three Poems," *Return to Default,* June 23, 2013, https://returntodefault.wordpress.com/2013/06/23/trevor-joyce-three-poems/.

row is fucking us up. Tomorrow is fucked. That sentiment was present before the crisis, but at the time people with what might be termed "negative thoughts" were frequently and viciously ridiculed. A famous example of this was delivered by Bertie Ahern. Ahern played a pivotal role in the Good Friday Agreement and presided over the Celtic Tiger era, but he was later forced to resign over suspicions around his personal finances. At the biennial conference of the Irish Congress of Trade Unions in Bundoran, County Donegal on July 4, 2007, Ahern addressed the trade union delegates. Speaking in front of cutouts of white figures encircling the globe in blue and pink and white, he warned delegates against a return to the wage-price inflationary spiral of the mid-1980s, Ahern assured Union leaders that the government was committed to the "social partnership" approach, which involved tripartite, triennial national pay agreements, in dealing with challenges to maintain the competitiveness of the Irish economy. Strike and wage moderation were important outcomes of the social partnership agreements, and this was viewed as a significant contributor to the Celtic Tiger. In his prepared remarks at Bundoran, the Taoiseach said:

> My message to you this morning is about confidence for the future. Confidence, in the strength of the economy that we have created together over recent decades. Confidence, in the value of the social progress which that economic strength has made possible. Confidence, in our own judgement in the face of commentators and others who regularly cast doubt, not only on our future, but even on the reality of our past achievements and how we managed to bring them about. [...] There are those who believe that our recent successes are an illusion. That they will disappear and we will be back to the natural order, an Ireland of unemployment and underachievement.[3]

---

3   Finfacts Team, "Taoiseach Expresses Surprise that 'Cribbing and Moaning' Critics of Irish Economy and Government Policy 'Don't Commit Suicide,'"

Ahern's statements embody the performative aspect of language; it is a legislative utterance about futurity and how to ensure a positive future. He does so by taking aim at people who talk down the economy, saying after the talk, "Sitting on the sidelines, cribbing and moaning is a lost opportunity. I don't know how people who engage in that don't commit suicide because frankly the only thing that motivates me is being able to actively change something."[4] Standing by the sentiment, he plamásed afterwards that it was a "bad choice of words." These words nonetheless make a few of the implicit assertions of the speech explicit and might be said to follow logically from the whole thrust of Ahern's remarks, that perhaps the seppuku of those who remain negative is a necessary condition for this ostensibly positive future.

Trevor Joyce's *The Immediate Future* is emphatically negative about the future, the one we now shiver inside. The chapbook, originally published by Rachel Warriner and James Cummins's RunAmok press in Cork, contains thirty-four poems in sequence. They explore the links between divination and economics in an attempt to recover from economists the role of prediction, in particular negative outcomes, with constant reference to prophecy and actuarial calculations. The thirty-first poem of *The Immediate Future* takes "futures" as its topic:

futures are
difficult

must be teased
out of the
wildness
of the living

sadness or

Finfacts, July 4, 2007, http://www.finfacts.ie/irelandbusinessnews/publish/article_1010514.shtml.

4   Ibid.

> undue panic
> in the beast
> is a distinct
> indicator
>
> should the
> ceremony
> discover
> flawed or
> terrifying
> flesh all bets
> are off[5]

Futures are contracts for assets (especially commodities or shares) bought at agreed prices but delivered and paid for later.[6] The poem says these are "difficult," but for whom? Well, they must be "teased / out" of the "living" — living here is all who live, and also "living" in the sense of a job. We cut then, in the poem, to a sacrifice (as a "beast" is killed in a "ceremony" to check its "flesh") — but is the "beast" a person, the body of a worker or the body of workers? Once a sacrifice is made, it is possible that the beast will be found to be monstrous or deformed inside, and this will mean "all bets are off." The reference to "flawed or terrifying flesh" is borrowed from the following text on divination and rituals in the Ancient world:

> In the *namburbis* the evil omens stem from flesh which is described as [...] "flawed or terrifying" flesh, or as [...] miss-

---

5   Trevor Joyce, *The Immediate Future*, 37.
6   Futures are "[c]ontracts made in a 'future market' for purchase or sale of commodities or financial assets, on a specified future date. Futures are negotiable instruments, i.e, they may be bought and sold. Many commodity exchanges (e.g. wool, cotton and wheat) have established futures markets that permit manufacturers and traders to hedge against changes in the price of raw materials they use or deal in" (Graham Bannock and R.E. Baxter, *The Penguin Dictionary of Economics* [London: Penguin, 2011], s.v. "Futures").

ing flesh. [...] Circumstances surrounding the performance of divination were themselves observed and interpreted as ominous signs, as we know was the case with the behavior of the sacrificed animal itself.[7]

The link being made between animal sacrifice and trading of futures puts forward an ostensibly perennialist argument that we must acknowledge the ways in which history rhymes across cultures, that somehow futures are a correlate to animal sacrifice but the animals are human beings, the laboring underclass. We need only think of the title of Lordan's collection *Invitation to a Sacrifice* alongside Joyce's poem. The force of the comparison does not imply any value judgement about this prophesying.

Before looking further into Joyce's chapbook, it may be worth discussing a prominent episode during the financial crisis in Ireland in which the financial instruments arranged to service a future income for retired workers, i.e., pensions, came under pressure.[8] On January 5, 2009 it was announced that Waterford Wedgewood was in receivership, and a sit-in began soon after at the Waterford Crystal factory in Kilbarry, Co. Waterford to fight the 480 redundancies. These workers, desperate to keep the factory going, continued to autonomously give tours of the factory to visiting tourists and sold ware from the factory shop. They wanted the government to nationalize the company and run it, or for the company to be bought and run as normal. But nationalizing assets rather than losses was anathema to the government. During the occupation, Waterford Crystal's pension scheme was said to be about €111 million in deficit, which had many workers also worrying about redundancy payments.

---

7 Ulla Susanne Koch, "Three Strikes and You're Out! A View on Cognitive Theory and the First-Millennium Extispicy Ritual," in *Divination and Interpretation of Signs in the Ancient World*, ed. Amar Annus (Chicago: Oriental Institute of the University of Chicago, 2010), 43–59, at 47. Available online at https://oi.uchicago.edu/sites/oi.uchicago.edu/files/uploads/shared/docs/ois6.pdf.
8 Kieran Allen, *Ireland's Economic Crash: A Radical Agenda for Change* (Dublin: Liffey, 2009), 1–2.

Prospective buyers included US private equity groups Clarion Capital and KPS Capital, but KPS made it clear that it had no intention of retaining jobs in Waterford, as it would only buy the brand name.[9] The occupiers enjoyed the solid support of the local community, with businesses and individuals in the area supplying food, water, and mattresses. The eight-week long workers' occupation ended with the workforce reluctantly accepting a deal. Waterford Crystal's assets were sold to KPS Capital Partners. A scaled-down House of Waterford Crystal was quickly built on Waterford's Mall, but most of the products it sells are made overseas.[10] Unite were engaged with the Labour Relations Commission to resolve the issue and give the former workers their payments. A case was brought against the Irish Government to the European Court of Justice, and this led to a ruling in April 2013 to the effect that it was up to the state to protect pension rights of employees whose payments had gone south, putting the ball firmly in the government's court. In 2013 the European Court of Justice ruled that the Irish state is in breach of its obligations under the terms of the EU Insolvency Directive to ensure that employees receive sufficient pension entitlements. Thousands of people took part in a protest in Waterford City on August 23, 2014 in solidarity with the former Waterford Crystal workers who are still awaiting their pensions, and many

---

9 Henry McDonald, "Waterford Staff's Crystal-clear Vision," *The Guardian*, February 22, 2009, https://www.theguardian.com/world/2009/feb/22/waterford-crystal-factory-sit-in-workers.

10 Conor Kane, "Waterford Crystal: How Cracks Appeared in the Recession," *The Irish Times*, December 14, 2014, https://www.irishtimes.com/news/social-affairs/waterford-crystal-how-cracks-appeared-in-the-recession-1.2037293. In 2013 Unite union argued to the Office for Harmonisation in the Internal Market, Europe's trademark registry that "Waterford Crystal" contains an implied geographical indication preventing the company from selling any goods it has produced outside Waterford ("Union Challenges Production of Waterford Crystal in Slovenia," *The Irish Times*, March 5, 2013, https://www.irishtimes.com/business/manufacturing/union-challenges-production-of-waterford-crystal-in-slovenia-1.1317407).

still awaited pensions in 2016.[11] The future of these workers was sacrificed for profitability.

Perhaps it is morbid to move from pension considerations to the rights of widows, but let's try. This is the twenty-third poem in Joyce's chapbook:

> prognosticators
> bring you
> cedarwood
>
> the widow
> offers roasted
> flour
>
> poor folk
> give oil
>
> the wealthy
> farmer from
> his flock
> selects
> a lamb
>
> all these
> to praise you
>
> that you may
> skew the probabilities
>
> fix the game[12]

---

[11] "Thousands Protest in Support of Former Waterford Crystal Workers," *The Irish Examiner,* August 23, 2014, https://www.irishexaminer.com/ireland/100-waterford-crystal-workers-still-waiting-for-pensions-385019.html.

[12] Joyce, *The Immediate Future,* 27.

Each brings something "to you" according to their resources. (Joyce is fond of the accusative second-person pronoun.) It is probably the diviner, the reader as actuary. The source text for this poem is a Mesopotamian prayer to the sun god Shamash. "The professional diviner brings you cedar resin, the widow roasted grain […] the poor woman oil, the wealthy man out of his wealth a lamb."[13] This prayer, another source notes, is said to avert bad dreams.[14] The poor widow can only offer grain, but in some ways gives more than the rich person who gives "out of his wealth."[15] Karen van der Toorn explains that widows were understood as a threat to a patriarchal order and as potential witches but also as the unprotected and underprivileged.[16] But the widow here is pious, devotional in her place of worship. You are brought a gift, a sacrifice, so that you can protect the figures in the poem, "fix the game" to ensure their success or survival. But how do "you" respond?

The grammatical form of the immediate future is composed of three elements: subject + the verb *to be,* conjugated in the present tense + about + the infinitive of the main verb. This pattern is used to refer to a time immediately after the moment of speaking and emphasizes that the event or action will happen very soon. It is not until the final stanza of the chapbook that the promised immediate future grammatical form appears: "things

---

13 Karen van der Toorn, "The Public Image of the Widow in Ancient Israel," in *Between Poverty and the Pyre: Moments in the History of Widowhood,* eds. Jan Bremmer and Lourens Van Den Bosch (London: Routledge, 2002), 19–30, at 25.
14 W.G. Lambert, "Donations of Food and Drink to the Gods in Ancient Mesopotamia," in *Ritual and Sacrifice in the Ancient Near East: Proceedings of the International Conference Organized by the Katholieke Universiteit Leuven from the 17th to the 20th of April 1991,* ed. Jan Quaegebeur (Leuven: Peeters, 1993), 191–201, at 198–99.
15 See Luke 21:1–4.
16 Karen van der Toorn, "Torn Between Vice and Virtue: Stereotypes of the Widow in Israel and Mesopotamia," in *Female Stereotypes in Religious Traditions,* eds. Ria Kloppenborg and Wouter J. Hanegraaff (Leiden: Brill, 1995), 9.

are / about to / get ugly." The final poem of the chapbook in full goes:

> make no
> mistake
>
> be under
> no illusion
>
> be clear
> about this
>
> let no-one
> fool them-
> selves
>
> we are
> where
> we are
>
> the cup-
> board's bare
>
> never for
> one moment
> imagine
>
> don't think
>
> things are
> about to get
> ugly[17]

This has a paternalist tone, offering advice in a pontificating manner. You, as the reader, must not "fool" yourself, and "we"

---

17 Joyce, *The Immediate Future*, 40.

are exactly where we are, there is nothing left in the cupboard. The situation, we are made to understand, is bad and will get worse. The line and stanza breaks here foster ambiguity and might thereby be said to interrogate prevalent economic and political sentiments or lean towards polemic, but even if ambiguity was useful at a particular historical moment (and right now it is not) it never fully occupies that tone in the way Warriner's *Eleven Days* does. The last two lines could be what we are being told not to think — *don't think that things are going to get worse*. In this, it holds close to Ahern's sentiment, though expressed less violently. Or it could be the poem's own prophecy — that things definitely are going to get worse. The options are: one, *Don't think that things are about to get worse* and two, *Don't think. Oh, also, things are about to get worse.* The gap between these options is not as wide as it appears at first. The effect of the first statement is akin to *don't think of an elephant* — its apparent meaning as an injunction is destroyed as it is uttered, since all one can now think of is an elephant.[18] The poem ventriloquizes the discourse of the politician enforcing economic realism (*realism* in the narrow sense, that only a certain spectrum of neoliberal policies are the only options on the table) by stopping thought (*don't think* in the imperative) and uttering tautologous dribble (*we are where we are*).[19] In Byrne's poems a rigid thought is made *pliant* again. In the final lines of *The Immediate Future,* no such strategy is pursued. The lines are toneless and vacant in comparison to those of Byrne's discussed in section 5, which are full of life, vivacity, wit, and resilience. Ryan's characters wrestle with clichés but continue to reside in them, defeated, and although Joyce's poem has no characters (rather, it is populated

---

18 James Butler, "How Politicians Used Metaphors to Sell Us Austerity," *Vice*, February 21, 2018, https://www.vice.com/en_uk/article/9kzng7/how-politicians-used-metaphors-to-sell-us-austerity.

19 On "we are where we are," see Sinéad Kennedy, "A Perfect Storm: Crisis, Capitalism and Democracy," in *Ireland under Austerity: Neoliberal Crises, Neoliberal Solution,* eds. Colin Coulter and Angela Nagle (Manchester: Manchester University Press, 2015), 86–109, at 98. See also page 12 of the same book.

with "types" such as actuaries and widows), it is similar in tone. Joyce's use of cliché is perhaps more quietist than Byrne, Ryan, or Warriner. But it also fizzes with a blizzard of implications, about the kind of worseness we're in for and how to exploit it, as these poets try to harness entropy for their own ends. In this gesture of Joyce's final poem lies a faint mimesis of the vacant housing estates that litter Ireland, an obliterated life free from hope and habituation.

6.1

The Decline and Fall of Whatever Empire

Daily there are declamations of a state of emergency, the falling of a new Dark Age. It seems likely that the age of liberal democracy is over. I would like to turn now to *The Immediate Future*'s seventh poem, which in full is:

day of
cleansing

men forget
their women

women their
children

the slate is
wiped clean

words rinsed
clear of old
associations

> all history
> obliterated
>
>
> occurrence of this
> climacteric
> is irregular and
> unpredictable
>
>
> must be
> professionally
> provoked[1]

There is a "day of / cleansing," and familial relations are forgotten, "the slate is / wiped clean" like an Etch-A-Sketch. The integrity of the family falls apart, perhaps widening (as in Rusangano *Family*), in a chain apparently patriarchal as "men forget / their women" and then "women their / children." The word "climacteric" in the fourteenth line is used to describe this "day of cleansing," and it is both an adjective and noun, "constituting or having the effect of a critical event or point in time; critical, decisive; epochal"[2] or a "critical period or moment in history, a person's life or career, etc."[3] In L.M. Cullen's *An Economic History of Ireland since 1660,* a chapter entitled "The Climacteric of the 1970s and 1980s" describes the consequences of an open economy that emerged dramatically in the '70s. There was a sharp increase in Ireland's prosperity in the '70s, but simultaneously the country's creditor status swung to debtor status.[4] The term "climacteric" also has a medical or physiological meaning: "of, relating to, or designating a period of physical (and, often, psychological) change occurring in middle age and believed to

---

1 Trevor Joyce, *The Immediate Future* (Dublin: Smithereens, 2017), 11.
2 *Oxford English Dictionary,* s.v. "climacteric," adj. 1.b.
3 Ibid., n., 1.
4 L.M. Cullen, *An Economic History of Ireland Since 1660* (London: Batsford, 1987), 186–87.

Fig. 5. Late Bronze Age ghost estate Eflatun Pınar on the cover of *The Immediate Future* (2017). See http://smithereenspress.com/publications/sp20.html. Cover photograph © Trevor Joyce.

indicate the onset of senescence."[5] Senescence of a country? Senescence of a culture? Senescence of capital? Brenner dates the long downturn to this same period. I would suggest that the climacteric in these lines which destroys and yet is part of history is caused by a particular profession, as the poem tells us it "must be / professionally / provoked," and in the context of the whole chapbook that profession is probably *actuary*—"actuarial circles" are mentioned in the thirty-first poem.

The Immediate Future was reissued as a free e-book by Smithereens Press in 2017, and this edition features a photograph

---

5 *Oxford English Dictionary*, s.v. "climacteric."

taken by Joyce of a Hittite monument at Eflatun Pınar in modern-day Turkey (see figure 5). One of the axes that Joyce's work thinks along is what is hyperbolically termed the rise and fall of empires and civilizations, also known as societal collapse. In cases of collapse, the wisdom runs, civilizations tend to revert to more complex, less centralized socio-political forms using simpler technology, often labelled a Dark Age. While collapse is often deplored, J.C. Scott points out "the situation it depicts is most often the disaggregation of a complex, fragile and oppressive state into smaller, decentralized fragments."[6] Embracing collapse is exactly what Joyce, Lordan, and Warriner do — why they might seem nihilistic. What looks like nihilism to a liberal commentator concerned with integration is embracing the dehiscence of a centralized power structure. Scott goes on: "far from being seen as regrettable backsliding and privation," and what is normally described as civilizational decline "may well have been experienced as a marked improvement" in many people's living conditions as their autonomy increases.[7] Such a disintegration may be relatively abrupt and disastrous, as in the case of Mayan civilization, or gradual, as in the case of the fall of the Western Roman Empire, a topic discussed in Joyce's *Rome's Wreck: Translated from the English of Edmund Spenser's Ruines of Rome* (2014) and *Fastness: A translation from the English of Edmund Spenser* (2017). The Hittite Empire, manufacturer of the ruin on the cover of Joyce's e-book, and the Han and Tang Dynasty of China which appeared in the poem "Capital Accounts," are examples of civilizations and societies which would be described as having collapsed by reversion or simplification at some point in time. Theodor W. Adorno's 1950 essay "Spengler after the Downfall" rereads Spengler's thesis on the decline of the West in light of the catastrophic destruction of Nazi Germany, noting that Spengler's insights were often more profound than those of his more liberal contemporaries. Adorno criticizes

---

6 James C. Scott, *Against the Grain: A Deep History of the Earliest States* (New Haven: Yale University Press, 2017), 209.
7 Ibid., 232.

6.1 THE DECLINE AND FALL OF WHATEVER EMPIRE

Spengler for an overly deterministic view of history, ignoring the unpredictable role that human initiative plays at all times. He notes that decay contains new opportunities for renewal, thereby harnessing doomsaying for the left. I think that this is what is happening in Joyce's work too. We are being asked to think about what ruins mean, what buildings mean when empty of people, to look at the consequences of capital flight, hinterlands built up and sucked dry and then emptied of human labor as soon as accumulation becomes easier elsewhere.

The ruined monument greeting us on the cover of Joyce's book recalls not only the real ghost estates that dot the country but some of Lordan's poetry. In particular the title and the cover image of the Smithereens Press online edition get us to think about the way in which the ruins of the future are also the ruins of the past, as in Lordan's "A Resurrection in Charlesland":

> Our imitation terracotta roofs can't wait to collapse on us
> cave in becoming overnight poetic and mysterious
> like all the slumped stone cottages they're jealous of
>   relics of so many oldsung irish hells
>   that memorise the bitter twisted centuries before us
>   and that we wist on whizzing by in cars or trains,
>
> lulled to a deep-thought serenity
> by their silent exterior stillness through the window-glass,
> as each of them weakly yet perceptibly
>   returns to us reflections
>   that our inheritance is the mirror of our legacy.[8]

There is a funny play on inheritance here in terms of what we get from the past but also what we might get in the event of the death of a relative. For Joyce's poetry, I think, the ruined façade from the Hittite Empire rhymes with the ghost estate, empty and unprofitable, vacant of wage-earners and emotion.

---

8 Lordan, *Invitation to a Sacrifice* (Clare: Salmon, 2010), 111. "Wist" is an onomatopoeic word, like *whoosh*.

In "The Holding Pattern," the collective Endnotes reads these empty buildings as a manifestation of "corruption." They were built because of corrupt deals which "appeared as corrupt only retrospectively: when the tourists stopped coming, the housing market collapsed and consumer spending declined."[9] Ireland has the benefit of both a bailout to banks and vacant estates to memorialize its period of prosperity. What looked like wealth was a con. Scores of book covers about the crisis in Ireland choose ghost estates, as well as titles — from William Wall's *Ghost Estate* (2011) to the edited collection *From Prosperity to Austerity* published in 2014.

Joyce's *The Immediate Future* covers similar territory to "Capital Accounts" by deepening his earlier explorations of contemporary Ireland and Chinese history, throwing good money after bad on the sunk capital of those earlier comparisons. It focuses on comparing prognostication in the context of contemporary economics and of ancient divination. Paul Romer has suggested that the discourse of economics dresses up guesses, estimations, and speculation in numbers, which he terms the "mathiness critique."[10] In Dierdre McCloskey's words, it is when numbers are used to suggest that their methodology is "scientific" when it is anything but.[11] Alan Jay Levinovitz's article "The New Astrology" suggests that modern economics is an irrational superstition by anecdotally linking astrology and economics and outlining the historical interdependence of mathematics and astrology. Levinovitz compares contemporary mistakes in investing money to a specific snake-oil industry — astral science in Early Imperial

---

9 "The Holding Pattern: The Ongoing Crisis and the Class Struggles of 2011–2013," *Endnotes* 3 (2013): 12–54, at 40, https://endnotes.org.uk/issues/3/en/endnotes-the-holding-pattern.
10 Paul M. Romer, "Mathiness in the Theory of Economic Growth," *American Economic Review: Papers & Proceedings* 105, no. 5 (2015): 89–93.
11 Deirdre N. McCloskey, *The Rhetoric of Economics* (Madison: University of Wisconsin Press, 1998). Cf. Robert H. Nelson, *Economics as Religion: From Samuelson to Chicago and Beyond* (University Park: Pennsylvania State University Press, 2001).

China.¹² At that time, advanced mathematics known as *li* models were applied to the movement of the stars, and correspondingly in our own day, our best mathematical instruments and labors are applied to market movements. Levinovitz notes that "despite collective faith that these models would improve the fate of the Chinese people, they did not."¹³ He goes on:

> Modern governments, universities and businesses underwrite the production of economic theory with huge amounts of capital. The same was true for li production in ancient China. Like many economic models today, li models were less important to practical affairs than their creators (and consumers) thought them to be.¹⁴

Economic theory is a colossal effort to assuage the ruling class that what is happening anyway is the correct thing to do, while its vast number of test subjects with varying degrees of calm wait in line for their defenestration. Joyce's sequence of poems silently quotes a variety of sources, mainly historical and anthropological, which discuss humanity's ancient cultural practices, in particular divination. The sequence puts forward an argument that is similar to Levinovitz's.

Chinese history (specifically early Chinese history, the Shang dynasty, 1600–1046 BCE) and Sinology are threaded through Joyce's account of historical and economic developments in Ireland. The Shang dynasty is the earliest dynasty of traditional Chinese history supported by archaeological evidence, and it occupied the Yellow River Valley in the second millennium BCE. A site at Anyang has yielded the earliest known body of Chinese writing, mostly divinations inscribed on "oracle bones" — main-

---

12 He relies on Daniel Patrick Morgan, *Astral Sciences in Early Imperial China: Observation, Sagehood and the Individual* (Cambridge: Cambridge University Press, 2017).
13 Alan Jay Levinovitz, "The New Astrology," *Aeon*, April 4, 2016, https://aeon.co/essays/how-economists-rode-maths-to-become-our-era-s-astrologers.
14 Ibid.

ly turtle shells and ox scapulae. The inscriptions provide critical insight into the politics, economy, religious practices, art, and medicine of this early stage of Chinese civilization. In Joyce's sequence a link is posited between archaic divination and the actuarial predictive techniques underlying derivatives. David N. Keightley's *The Ancestral Landscape* (2000) and some of Keithley's other published work are key sources for several of the poems in *The Immediate Future*.

Divination is the attempt to gain insight into a question or situation by way of a standardized process or ritual. The Shang dynasty engaged in divination through scapulamancy and plastromancy—the following quote from Keightley is a good summary of this ritual:

Shang plastromancy and scapulimancy […] proceeded as follows. A topic was addressed to the turtle shell or bone in the form of a charge, which was frequently couched in either alternative (A or B) or in positive and negative (A not A) modes. Thus, an initial inquiry about millet harvest might be divided into the two contrasting charges, "We will receive millet harvest" […] and "We may not receive millet harvest" […]. The charges were thus tentative predictions or statements of intent, proclaimed to the spirits for their approval or disapproval. Single, unpaired charges, which, as we shall see, became more common with the passage of time, were prediction, even wishes—"In the next ten days there will be no disaster" […], for example—divined in order to test the reaction of the spirits. As the charge was addressed to the shell or bone, a hot bronze poker or some other heat source was applied to a series of hollows or pits that had already been bored or chiselled into its back; the heat caused T-shaped stress cracks to form, with up to ten cracks being made in ten separate hollows for each question. Having been numbered and examined, the cracks, and thus the charges with which they were associated, were interpreted, if possible, as lucky or unlucky to a greater or lesser degree.[15]

The act of divination was performed to avert disasters.

An actuary is a person "trained in the calculation of risk and premiums for assurance purposes."[16] Actuarial science is the discipline that applies mathematical and statistical methods to assess risk in insurance, finance, and other industries and professions. Joyce's poem smashes these actuaries into the found-language of Keightley's descriptions of Shang China. This link between ancient religion and contemporary finance culture has a strong whiff of perennialism, and the chapbook relishes taking that risk. In the thirty-first poem, a number of scenarios are sketched out which would upset a circle of actuaries, because they strike them as "calamities":

incursions
of a hunting
king

enemy
assaults

voracious
birds and
insects

onslaughts
of wind
rain drought
or flood

---

15 David N. Keightley, *These Bones Shall Rise Again: Selected Writings on Early China,* ed. Henry Rosemont Jr. (New York: State University of New York Press, 2014), 123–25.

16 Graham Bannock and R.E. Baxter, *The Penguin Dictionary of Economics* (London: Penguin, 2011), s.v. "Actuary."

entering
abruptly
at one
horizon

exiting
haphazardly

there is now
no appetite
for such
calamities
in actuarial
circles[17]

The poem lists bad weather, animal swarms, enemies, and the king's hunting expeditions as possible mishaps or disturbances to something like a baseline-normalcy. The line "entering abruptly at one horizon" is taken from the following text, which implies that the above "king" is a Shang dynasty king:

> Many inhabitants of Shang China would have had little notion of the land that lay beyond their daily horizon. Travelling no further than their local fields and woods, many peasants would have felt themselves at the center of a small familiar world that was intermittently and unpredictably invaded by external forces—like the king on hunt or campaign, marauding beasts, enemy raiders, voracious birds and insects, and, above all, the onslaughts of wind, rain, drought, and flood—that entered, often abruptly and unpredictably, from one horizon, left their mark on a settlement, and then passed out of its ken.[18]

---

17 Joyce, *The Immediate Future*, 35.
18 David N. Keightley, *The Ancestral Landscape: Time, Space, and Community in Late Shang China (ca. 1200–1045 B.C.)* (Berkeley: Institute of East Asian Studies, 2000), 55.

The uncertainty of the Shang peasantry is contrasted to that of a group of actuaries. What is it that links the Shang administration to actuarial practices? Well, partly the answer lies in the word "administration," as the term and cognates surface repeatedly in Keightley's account of the Shang. He states that in the late Shang an "elite minority of administrators, warriors, and religious figures was controlling, and benefitting from, the labors of the rest of the population."[19] The Shang also had a "proto-bureaucratic" attitude towards the supernatural.[20] In China, Keightley claims, the lord is "not the hero" but an "administrator."[21] The actuaries find the uncertainty of the peasant life intolerable, the two mindsets cannot coexist. In the *longue durée,* smoothing out spikes of uncertainty into calming bell curves is the historical march that brings us to where we are. The question becomes: are we going to become like the Shang peasants, unadministrable? Or are we already akin to them? When reading the chapbook, it is not immediately clear how Joyce's stance might differ from that sketched out in financier Peter L. Bernstein's *Against the Gods* (1996), which gives an overview of the development of risk management, ending with options and derivatives. Bernstein, himself a member of the priestly caste of financial consultants, posits that this is a progression from prophesying and the power of a priestly caste to increasing democratization and more rational decision making. Nonetheless, systemic risk becomes more of an issue as he finishes, and he notes that it is possible that a new brand of computer-augmented soothsayers has simply replaced human ones, bringing with them more obscure forms of fallibility and bias.[22] But let's turn to a poem to find out.

The eighth poem of *The Immediate Future* is the following:

early foresight
comprehends

---

19 Keightley, *These Bones Shall Rise Again*, 1.
20 Ibid., 54.
21 Ibid., 41.
22 Peter L. Bernstein, *Against the Gods: The Remarkable Story of Risk* (New York: John Wiley, 1996).

the king's
health

his hunts
his dreams
those cities
he constructed

his income
and his absolute
decrees

theological
constriction
follows

life-events
interrogated
shrink
in range

negative outcomes
are not entertained

all is
auspicious[23]

This poem opens with "foresight," the ability to see the future, predicting or comprehending the "king's hunt" which another poem postulated as an upset to the orderly running of day-to-day life for actuaries. The final word might be momentarily misread as "suspicious", perhaps even mistyped — "A" and "S" are next to each other on the QWERTY keyboard. The content here closely follows a section of an essay by Edward Shaughnessy discussing the Shang dynasty in China:

---

23 Joyce, *The Immediate Future*, 12.

6.1 THE DECLINE AND FALL OF WHATEVER EMPIRE

By the end of the Shang dynasty, something of a theological constriction took place in the Shang kings' performance of divination. No longer was the broad range of royal life open to determination, nor were negative consequences entertained.[24]

Joyce has taken the words "theological constriction" and changed "consequences" to "outcomes." The "theological / constriction" implies that the king is attempting to limit the divine, getting too big for his boots, too big to fail. Discussing this tendency, Keightley says:

Shang divination was losing its "working" nature by the closing reigns of the dynasty. If no bad forecasts were to be recorded, there would have been no need to record crack notations either. These trends all represent a routinization and simplification of the divination process, a paring away of time-consuming procedures, and, inevitably, a change in man's religious and metaphysical assumptions.[25]

As Keightly says, acts of divination became "spells applied to the future" or "attempts to make sure that there would be no disasters."[26] Shang divination and clichés have a mutual relationship here. The echoes with the rhetoric surrounding the economic crisis are obvious, in which nay-sayers were ignored or put down by economists and politicians alike. In the most extreme example of this, Bertie Ahern wondered aloud why such people didn't kill themselves. Ahern's admonitions, and the platitudes offered to soften austerity were spells cast on the future which need to be broken with counter-hexes. The above poem offers a pretty top-down overview of what is happening, baldly stating that foresight, in terms of financial instruments, is

---

24 Edward Shaughnessy, "The Religion of Ancient China," in *A Handbook of Ancient Religions*, ed. John R. Hinnells (Cambridge: Cambridge University Press, 2007), 490–536, at 526.
25 Keightley, *These Bones Shall Rise Again*, 136.
26 Ibid., 127–28.

no longer working if everything is constantly stated to be auspicious or going well. Joyce's poetry does not want a temporary stay of the future, it does not forestall but beckons it forth. What we have in this poetry, in the work of Joyce and Lordan and Warriner, is not a cruel optimism, but a compassionate pessimism, one thread of the tantric screed which calls for a better end of the world. It is precisely the powerlessness of the cliché with which Joyce's final poem ends ("things are / about to get / ugly") that we must meditate on, as discussed in section 6. This cliché is inept and weak in the face of the compelling and jolting juxtapositions which this poetry has up to now put before us. This poetry has been forcing us to think more obscurely, laterally, to pay attention to absences and shifts which must of necessity be brought into the open by virtue of what is stated on the page.

The excellent critic Joe Cleary begins his assessment of Irish literary reactions to the crisis by observing that national literatures can die. They can, but any national literature was a funeral march all along, each author no sooner canonized than embalmed, whether living or dead. Cleary rightly points out that much literature produced in Ireland during the second half of the twentieth century has remained "transfixed" at a certain point in time, with "established" writers repeatedly locating their fictions in de Valera's Ireland of the 1930s, '40s and '50s.[27] Cleary is surprised that "the relationship between the political establishment and the artistic one remained, before and after the crash, essentially affable and noncontentious."[28] But his argument can look rather circular when one considers that he is looking for "an artistic masterpiece" from the literary "establishment." How can anyone be shocked that, for example, Colm Tóibín is so complicit in the neoliberal apparatus as to defend bankers and suggest literature can attract investment from abroad in Ireland? Having wandered into the butcher, Cleary is furious to discover

---

27 Joe Cleary, "'Horseman, Pass By!' The Neoliberal World System and the Crisis in Irish Literature," *boundary 2* 45, no. 1 (2017): 135–79, at 139–40.
28 Ibid., 140, 142.

there are no cakes available. Cleary holds that the response to the Crisis has been "muted" and "pragmatic," but this does a disservice to many Irish writers, including Joyce, Lordan, and Warriner.[29] One cannot find the species of response Cleary is looking for in a Waterstones or put out by a large publisher, but small-press publishers provide some inkling of the real dissent. The only mainstream publication I have cited appears to exhibit the most reactionary thinking.

Every poem is thoroughly of the world, damaged and fucked up by it, and there are profound lessons in that damage. What binds all of these poems is that they refuse to wash behind their ears. The Irish navy has a Samuel Beckett-class offshore patrol vessel, but there will never be an LÉ Lordan or LÉ Warriner.[30] This is partly because of the future of the nation-state and the way it latched onto certain writers via their passports. It is also due to the historical situation these writers find themselves in, one in which nations are cowed under by multinational conglomerates and supra-state actors. In October 2014 the first post-bailout budget introduced tax cuts, and following criticism from the US and EU closed a loophole that allowed foreign multinationals to pay very low tax. In August 2016 the European Commission ordered Ireland to recover up to €13 billion in back taxes from Apple, after ruling that the firm had been receiving illegal state aid. The Irish government appealed against the ruling on the grounds that it would harm job creation and investment. The Irish government has continued to claw desperately for a slice of a declining pie — as opportunities for profit shrink. In the work of Joyce and Lordan and Warriner, it is clear that there is no future other than the future of futures, which must be refused, though they are refused to us. The pie will continue to shrink insofar as it is measured and we're going to have to deal with it. Things *are* ugly.

---

29 Ibid., 171.
30 Óglaigh na hÉireann / Irish Defence Forces, "LÉ Samuel Beckett," *YouTube*, May 17, 2014. https://www.youtube.com/watch?v=npbglEGYRsI.

The poems I have discussed are extremely important, but they are also fragile, distorted, stunted. The importance of this work is not lessened by how fucked up and damaged (and in some cases, such as Flynn's poem, reactionary) they are, by how this spins their readers out. We must care all the more for them because of this. We want no luminaries, which would simply continue the baleful funeral march of living greats. Stature is not our concern but laying low. These poets, these voices, in chorus, get at all the ways in which contemporary life is buckled under the pressure of news cycles and financial gain, and do so in failure and despair, the despair of chucking their own work out the window, as in Byrne's "fuckit," and in the weird gaps and occlusions these poems bring into relief, and that failure cannot itself be stupidly elevated to a new triumph. They are not building social imaginaries in antecedence of any social movements but following and working alongside those movements. Some critics would kneejerk-opine that these texts don't go far enough, could push further, that they remain in the bowels of whatever it is they think they criticize. It is a common trope in Irish studies to mourn like this, haunted by the putatively more advanced work from centers of empire. Well, I don't really care that these poems are fucked and remain constrained by the hegemonic imaginaries of their peripheral present, nor am I saddened that they are wounded by history or might be read as more muted than some tub-thumping poems from elsewhere, because literature is not escape. This is what we have, this is part of what there is.

Bibliography

"About." BLOCK T. https://www.blockt.ie/about.
"A History of Separation: The Defeat of the Workers' Movement." *Endnotes* 4 (2015): 70–192. https://endnotes.org.uk/issues/4/en/endnotes-preface.
Allen, Kieran. *Ireland's Economic Crash: A Radical Agenda for Change*. Dublin: Liffey, 2009.
Amadeo, Kimberly. "Iceland's Economy, Its Bankruptcy, and the Financial Crisis: How a Volcanic Eruption Helped Iceland Recover." *the balance*, May 30, 2019. https://www.thebalance.com/iceland-financial-crisis-bankruptcy-and-economy-3306347.
"Anglo Irish to Change Name as Part of Long Exit." *Reuters*, July 1, 2011. https://uk.reuters.com/article/angloirishbank/anglo-irish-to-change-name-as-part-of-long-exit-idUKL6E7I110Q20110701.
An Roinn Ealaíon, Oidhreachta agus Gaeltachta · Department of Arts, Heritage and the Gaeltacht. *Value for Money and Policy Review of the Arts Council*. 2015. https://www.chg.gov.ie/app/uploads/2015/09/value-for-money-and-policy-review-of-the-arts-council.pdf.
An Roinn Ealaíon, Oidhreachta, Gnóthaí, Réigiúnacha, Tuaithe agus Gaeltachta · Department of Arts, Heritage, Regional, Rural and Gaeltacht Affairs. *Culture 2025 — Éire Ildánach:*

A Framework Policy to 2025. 2016. https://www.chg.gov.ie/app/uploads/2016/07/culture_2025_framework_policy_document.pdf.

AP+E/Urban-Agency. "Shan-Zhen: How a Small Irish Town Influenced the Mega-City Shenzhen." *Arch Daily,* January 26, 2016. https://www.archdaily.com/780950/shan-zhen-the-unlikely-influence-of-a-small-irish-town-on-mega-city-shenzhen.

Appleton, Kate. "True. Right Down to My Ghost. The Donal Ryan Interview." *Three Monkeys Online.* http://www.threemonkeysonline.com/donal-ryan-interview/.

Arrighi, Giovanni. "Globalization and Historical Macrosociology." In *Sociology for the Twenty-First Century: Continuities and Cutting Edges,* edited by Janet Abu-Lughod, 117–33. Chicago: Chicago University Press 2000.

———. "Globalization, State Sovereignty, and the 'Endless' Accumulation of Capital." In *States and Sovereignty in the Global Economy,* edited by David A. Smith, Dorothy Solinge, and Steven C. Topik, 53–73. London: Routledge, 1997.

Arthur, Charles. "A Tiny Irish Town and China's Rise to Superpower Status: The UNIDO Connection." *UNIDO,* March 2, 2017. https://www.unido.org/stories/tiny-irish-town-and-chinas-rise-superpower-status.

Auden, W.H. *Collected Longer Poems.* London: Faber, 2012.

———. *Secondary Worlds.* London: Faber, 1968.

——— and Louise MacNeice. *Letters from Iceland.* London: Faber, 1985 [1937].

Austen, Jane. *Emma.* Middlesex: Penguin, 1968 [1816].

Bannock, Graham, and R.E. Baxter. *The Penguin Dictionary of Economics.* London: Penguin, 2011.

Berlant, Lauren. *Cruel Optimism.* Durham: Duke University Press, 2011.

Bernstein, Peter L. *Against the Gods: The Remarkable Story of Risk.* New York: John Wiley, 1996.

Bowers, Simon. "How One Irish Woman Made $22bn for Apple in a Year." *The Guardian,* May 29, 2013. https://www.

theguardian.com/technology/2013/may/29/apple-ireland-cork-cathy-kearney.

Brawn, Derek. *Ireland's House Party: What the Estate Agents Don't Want You to Know.* Dublin: Gill & Macmillan, 2009.

Brearton, Fran. "Profit and Loss by Leontia Flynn — Review." *The Guardian,* September 2, 2011. https://www.theguardian.com/books/2011/sep/02/profit-loss-leontia-flynn-review.

Brenner, Robert. "What Is Good for Goldman Sachs Is Good for America: The Origins of the Current Crisis." 2009. https://escholarship.org/uc/item/0sg0782h.

Brouillette, Sarah. *Literature and the Creative Economy.* Stanford: Stanford University Press, 2014.

Brown, Pamela. "Women at Work: 40 Years of Change." *The Irish Times,* June 8, 2013. https://www.irishtimes.com/life-and-style/people/women-at-work-40-years-of-change-1.1420721.

Butler, James. "How Politicians Used Metaphors to Sell Us Austerity." *Vice,* February 21, 2018. https://www.vice.com/en_uk/article/9kzng7/how-politicians-used-metaphors-to-sell-us-austerity.

Byrne, Elaine A. *Political Corruption in Ireland 1922–2010: A Crooked Harp?* Manchester: Manchester University Press, 2012.

Byrne, Mairéad. *You Have to Laugh, New + Selected Poems.* New York: Barrow Street Press, 2013.

Carswell, Simon. *Anglo Republic: Inside the Bank that Broke Ireland.* Dublin: Penguin, 2011.

"Celtic Tiger Prosperity and Immigration Go 'Hand in Paw,' Says Oracle's Chief." *Independent,* July 7, 2005. https://www.independent.ie/business/irish/celtic-tiger-prosperity-and-immigration-go-hand-in-paw-says-oracles-chief-25974378.html.

Central Statistics Office · An Phríomh-Oifig Staidrimh. "Population and Migration Estimates April 2003 (with Revisions to April 1997 and April 2002)." December 10, 2003. http://www.cso.ie/en/media/csoie/

releasespublications/documents/population/2003/
popmig_2003.pdf.

Chambers, Samuel A. *There's No Such Thing as "The Economy": Essays on Capitalist Value.* Earth: punctum books, 2018.

Clancy, Sarah. *Truth & Other Stories.* Clare: Salmon, 2011.

Cleary, Joe. "'Horseman, Pass By!': The Neoliberal World System and the Crisis in Irish Literature." *boundary 2* 45, no. 1 (2017): 135–79. DOI: 10.1215/01903659-4295527.

Cleary, Laurence, and Donal Ryan. "How I Write." Interview transcript. http://www.ulsites.ul.ie/rwc/sites/default/files/rwc_Donal_Ryan_How_I_Write%2BInterview_transcript.pdf.

Coakley, Maurice. *Ireland in the World Order: A History of Uneven Development.* London: Pluto, 2012.

Connor, Steven. "Beckett and the World." Lecture, Global Beckett Conference, Odense, October 26, 2006. http://stevenconnor.com/beckettworld.html.

Coulter, Colin. "Ireland under Austerity: An Introduction to the Book." In *Ireland under Austerity: Neoliberal Crises, Neoliberal Solutions,* edited by Colin Coulter and Angela Nagle, 1–43. Manchester: Manchester University Press, 2015.

Cullen, Paul, "Review of Report that Made Corruption Finding Against Burke." *The Irish Times,* November 23, 2015. https://www.irishtimes.com/news/environment/review-of-report-that-made-corruption-finding-against-burke-1.2414649.

Cunningham, Grainne. "How to Hire the Right Au Pair." *Independent,* July 12, 2013. https://www.independent.ie/life/family/mothers-babies/how-to-hire-the-right-au-pair-29411967.html.

Davis, John Francis. *Poeseos Sinicae Commentarii: The Poetry of the Chinese.* London: Asher, 1870 [1829].

Denny, Kevin, and Cormac Ó Gráda. *Irish Attitudes to Immigration during and after the Boom.* Dublin: University College Dublin Geary Institute, 2013.

Dolven, Jeff, and Joshua Kotin. "The Art of Poetry No. 101: J.H. Prynne." *Paris Review* 218 (2016): 174–207. https://www.

theparisreview.org/interviews/6807/j-h-prynne-the-art-of-poetry-no-101-j-h-prynne.

Dowling, Brian, "Ex-minister on Pension of €66,000." *Independent,* November 27, 2003. https://www.independent.ie/irish-news/exminister-on-pension-of-66000-25923785.html.

Duhigg, Charles, and David Kocieniewski, "How Apple Sidesteps Billions in Global Taxes." *New York Times,* April 28, 2012. https://www.pulitzer.org/files/2013/explanatory-reporting/04ieconomy4-29.pdf.

Dundon, T., M. Gonzalez-Perez, and T. Mc Donough. "Bitten by the Celtic Tiger: Immigrant Workers and Industrial Relations in the New Glocalised Ireland." *Economic and Industrial Democracy* 28, no. 4 (2007): 501–22. DOI: 10.1177/0143831X07082122.

Eliot, T.S. *The Waste Land,* in *Collected Poems 1909–1962,* 52–76. London: Faber, 2002.

Engels, Friedrich. *The Conditions of the Working Class in England.* Oxford: Oxford University Press, 2009 [1845]. https://www.marxists.org/archive/marx/works/download/pdf/condition-working-class-england.pdf.

Espeland, Wendy Nelson, and Mitchell L. Stevens. "Commensuration as a Social Process." *Annual Review of Sociology* 24 (1998): 313–43. DOI: 10.1146/annurev.soc.24.1.313.

"Eurozone Agrees €85bn Deal for Ireland." *RTÉ.* November 29, 2010. https://www.rte.ie/news/2010/1128/294894-economy/.

Ex, Kris. "Songs We Love: Rusangano Family, 'Heathrow.'" *American National Public Radio,* December 1, 2015. http://www.npr.org/2015/12/01/457924848/songs-we-love-rusangano-family-heathrow.

Falci, Eric. "Joinery: Trevor Joyce's Lattice Poems." In *Essays on the Poetry of Trevor Joyce,* edited by Niamh O'Mahony, 128–54. Bristol: Shearsman, 2015.

Fanning, Bryan. "Immigration, the Celtic Tiger and the Economic Crisis." *Irish Studies Review* 24 (2016): 9–20. DOI: 10.7765/9781526109279.00020.

Fenollosa, Ernest. *The Chinese Written Character as a Medium for Poetry: A Critical Edition.* New York: Fordham University Press, 2008.

Figes, Orlando. *Revolutionary Russia, 1891–1991.* London: Penguin, 2014.

Finfacts Team. "Taoiseach Expresses Surprise that 'Cribbing and Moaning' Critics of Irish Economy and Government Policy 'Don't Commit Suicide.'" *Finfacts Ireland,* July 4, 2007. http://www.finfacts.ie/irelandbusinessnews/publish/article_1010514.shtml.

Finn, Dan. "Ireland on the Turn?" *New Left Review* 67 (2011): 5–39. https://newleftreview.org/issues/II67/articles/daniel-finn-ireland-on-the-turn.

FitzGerald, Garret. "What Caused the Celtic Tiger Phenomenon?" *The Irish Times,* July 21, 2007. https://www.irishtimes.com/opinion/what-caused-the-celtic-tiger-phenomenon-1.950806.

Flynn, Leontia. "What Do I Know? (Or, Why I Need to Give up Post-modernism and Live an Irony-free Life)." *Edinburgh Review.* 2011. https://edinburgh-review.com/extracts/article-leontia-flynn/.

———. *Profit and Loss.* London: Cape, 2011.

Fourcade, Marion. "Theories of Markets and Theories of Society." *American Behavioral Scientists* 50 (2007): 1015–34. DOI: 10.1177/0002764207299351.

Frankel, Hans. H. *Flowering Plum and the Palace Lady: Interpretations of Chinese Poetry.* New Haven: Yale University Press, 1976.

Gaynor, Fergal. "Still Man: The Human as Unvoiced in the Poetry of Trevor Joyce." In *Essays on the Poetry of Trevor Joyce,* edited by Niamh O'Mahony, 53–80. Bristol: Shearsman, 2015.

Geary, Brendan. "Shattered Assumptions: A Tale of Two Traumas." In *From Prosperity to Austerity: A Socio-cultural Critique of the Celtic Tiger and Its Aftermath,* 47–61. Manchester: Manchester University Press, 2014.

Ging, Debbie. "All-consuming Images: New Gender Formations in Post-Celtic-Tiger Ireland." In *Transforming Ireland: Challenges, Critiques, Resource,* edited by Debbie Ging, Michael Cronin, and Peadar Kirby, 52–70. Manchester: Manchester University Press, 2009.

Gira, Melissa. *Playing the Whore.* London: Verso, 2014.

Goodman, Conor. "New Stars of Irish fiction: Did 'The Guardian' Get It Right?" *The Irish Times,* October 20, 2015. https://www.irishtimes.com/culture/books/new-stars-of-irish-fiction-did-the-guardian-get-it-right-1.2397659.

Gunne, Sorcha. "Contemporary Caitlín: Gender and Society in Celtic Tiger Popular Fiction." *Études littéraires* 37, no. 2 (2012): 143–58. DOI: 10.4000/etudesirlandaises.3202.

Hardy, Thomas. *Tess of D'Urbervilles.* London: Penguin, 2003 [1891].

Harvey, David. *A Brief History of Neoliberalism.* Oxford: Oxford University Press, 2007.

———. "Globalization in Question." *Rethinking Marxism* 8, no. 4 (1995): 1–17. DOI: 10.1080/08935699508685463.

Haughey, Nuala. "101 Held after Raids on Lap-dancing Clubs." *The Irish Times,* June 7, 2003. https://www.irishtimes.com/news/101-held-after-raids-on-lap-dancing-clubs-1.361662.

Hewison, Robert. *Cultural Capital: The Rise and Fall of Creative Britain.* London: Verso, 2014.

Jordan, Justine. "A New Irish Literary Boom: The Post-crash Stars of Fiction." *The Guardian,* October 17, 2015. https://www.theguardian.com/books/2015/oct/17/new-irish-literary-boom-post-crash-stars-fiction.

———. "The Spinning Heart by Donal Ryan — Review." *The Guardian,* November 28, 2013. https://www.theguardian.com/books/2013/nov/28/spinning-heart-donal-ryan-review.

Joyce, Trevor. *Selected Poems 1967–2014.* Bristol: Shearsman, 2014.

———. *The Immediate Future.* Cork: RunAmok, 2013.

———. *The Immediate Future.* Dublin: Smithereens, 2017.

———. "Three Poems." *Return to Default,* June 23, 2013. https://returntodefault.wordpress.com/2013/06/23/trevor-joyce-three-poems/.

———. *What's in Store: Poems, 200–2007.* Dublin: New Writers' Press; Toronto: The Gig, 2007.

Kane, Conor. "Thousands Protest in Support of Former Waterford Crystal Workers." *The Irish Examiner,* August 23, 2014. https://www.irishexaminer.com/ireland/100-waterford-crystal-workers-still-waiting-for-pensions-385019.html.

——— "Waterford Crystal: How Cracks Appeared in the Recession." *The Irish Times,* December 14, 2014. https://www.irishtimes.com/news/social-affairs/waterford-crystal-how-cracks-appeared-in-the-recession-1.2037293.

Kappala-Ramsamy, Gemma. "Debut Author: Donal Ryan." *The Guardian,* January 13, 2013. https://www.theguardian.com/books/2013/jan/13/donal-ryan-interview-spinning-heart.

Kassebaum, Gayathri Rajapur. "Karnatak Raga." In *The Garland Encyclopaedia of World Music,* edited by Alison Arnold, 115–35. New York: Taylor & Francis, 2000.

Katko, Justin. "Annotated Worksheet on Hot White Andy." In *Crisis Inquiry: A Special Volume of Damn the Caesars with Attention to the Work of Rob Halpern & Keston Sutherland,* edited by Richard Owens, 271–98. Scarborough: Punch Press, 2012.

Keatinge, Benjamin. "The Language of Globalization in Contemporary Irish Poetry." *Studi Irlandesi: A Journal of Irish Studies* 4 (2014): 69–84. DOI: 10.13128/SIJIS-2239–3978–14307.

Keightley, David N. *The Ancestral Landscape: Time, Space, and Community in Late Shang China (ca. 1200–1045 B.C.).* Berkeley: Institute of East Asian Studies, 2000.

———. *These Bones Shall Rise Again: Selected Writings on Early China,* edited by Henry Rosemont Jr. New York: State University of New York Press, 2014.

Kennard, Matt, and Claire Provost. "Story of cities #25: Shannon — A Tiny Irish Town Inspires China's Economic

Boom." *The Guardian,* April 19, 2016. https://www.theguardian.com/cities/2016/apr/19/story-of-cities-25-shannon-ireland-china-economic-boom.

Kennedy, Sinéad. "A Perfect Storm: Crisis, Capitalism and Democracy." In *Ireland under Austerity: Neoliberal Crises, Neoliberal Solution,* edited by Colin Coulter and Angela Nagle, 86–109. Manchester: Manchester University Press, 2015.

Kirby, Peadar, *Celtic Tiger in Collapse: Explaining the Weaknesses of the Irish Model.* London: Palgrave Macmillan, 2010.

———, Luke Gibbons, and Michael Cronin. *Reinventing Ireland: Culture, Society and the Global Economy.* London: Pluto Press, 2002.

Koch, Ulla Susanne. "Three Strikes and You're Out! A View on Cognitive Theory and the First-millennium Extispicy Ritual." In *Divination and Interpretation of Signs in the Ancient World,* edited by Amar Annus, 43–59. Chicago: Oriental Institute of the University of Chicago, 2010.

Lambert, W.G. "Donations of Food and Drink to the Gods in Ancient Mesopotamia." In *Ritual and Sacrifice in the Ancient Near East: Proceedings of the International Conference Organized by the Katholieke Universiteit Leuven from the 17th to the 20th of April 1991,* edited by Jan Quaegebeur, 191–201. Leuven: Peeters, 1993.

Lentin, Ronit. "Asylum Seekers, Ireland, and the Return of the Repressed." *Irish Studies Review* 24, no. 1 (2016): 21–34.

Levinovitz, Alan Jay. "The New Astrology." *Aeon.* April 4, 2016. https://aeon.co/essays/how-economists-rode-maths-to-become-our-era-s-astrologers.

Lloyd, David. "Rome's Wreck: Joyce's Baroque." In *Essays on the Poetry of Trevor Joyce,* edited by Niamh O'Mahony, 170–94. Bristol: Shearsman, 2015.

Lordan, Dave. *Invitation to a Sacrifice.* Clare: Salmon, 2010.

———. *The Word in Flames.* 2016.

Lucey, Anne, "Europe 'Amazed' at Steps Taken in Budget: Lenihan." *The Irish Times,* April 27, 2009. https://www.

irishtimes.com/business/europe-amazed-at-steps-taken-in-budget-lenihan-1.754167.

Mac Ruairi, Tomas. "Redmond Found Guilty of Planning Corruption." *Irish Independent,* November 20 2003. https://www.independent.ie/irish-news/redmond-found-guilty-of-planning-corruption-25922956.html

Marklew, Naomi. "The Future of Northern Irish Poetry: Fragility, Contingency, Value and Beauty." *English Academy Review* 31, no. 2 (2014): 64–80. DOI: 10.1080/10131752.2014.965419.

Marx, Karl. "Outline of a Report on the Irish Question to the Communist Educational Association of German Workers in London." December 16, 1867. https://www.marxists.org/archive/marx/works/1867/12/16.htm.

McCabe, Conor. "False Economy: The Financialisation of Ireland and the Roots of Austerity." In *Ireland under Austerity: Neoliberal Crisis, Neoliberal Solutions,* edited by Colin Coulter and Angela Nagle, 47–65. Manchester: Manchester University Press, 2015.

———. *The Sins of the Father: The Decisions that Shaped the Irish Economy.* Dublin: The History Press, 2013.

McCloskey, Deirdre N. *The Rhetoric of Economics.* Madison: University of Wisconsin Press, 1998.

McDonald, Frank. "George Redmond Among Most Corrupt Officials in Irish History." *The Irish Times,* February 20, 2016. https://www.irishtimes.com/news/ireland/irish-news/george-redmond-among-most-corrupt-officials-in-irish-history-1.2541848.

McDonald, Henry. "Waterford Staff's Crystal-clear Vision." *The Guardian,* February 22, 2009. https://www.theguardian.com/world/2009/feb/22/waterford-crystal-factory-sit-in-workers.

Mercille, Julien. *The Political Economy and Media Coverage of the European Economic Crisis: The Case of Ireland.* London: Routledge, 2015.

Mills, Mary Beth. "Gender and Inequality in the Global Labor Force." *Annual Review of Anthropology* 32 (2003): 41–62. DOI: 10.1146/annurev.anthro.32.061002.093107.

"Minister Defends Sex Trade Raids by Gardai." *The Irish Times*, October 2, 2003. https://www.irishtimes.com/news/minister-defends-sex-trade-raids-by-gardai-1.380158.

Monier-Williams, Monier. *A Sanskrit–English Dictionary: Etymologically and Philologically Arranged with Special Reference to Cognate Indo-European Languages*. Revised by E. Leumann, C. Cappeller, et al. Oxford: Clarendon Press, 1899.

Morgan, Daniel Patrick. *Astral Sciences in Early Imperial China: Observation, Sagehood and the Individual*. Cambridge: Cambridge University Press, 2017.

Moten, Fred. "The Subprime and the Beautiful." *African Identities* 11, no. 2 (2013): 237–45. DOI: 10.1080/14725843.2013.797289.

Mulhall, Anne. "Mind Yourself: Well-being and Resilience as Governmentality in Contemporary Ireland." *The Irish Review* 53 (2017): 29–44.

Nealon, Christopher. *The Matter of Capital: Poetry and Crisis in the American Century*. Cambridge: Harvard University Press, 2011.

Nelson, Robert H. *Economics as Religion: From Samuelson to Chicago and Beyond*. University Park: Pennsylvania State University Press, 2001.

Neveling, Patrick. "Export Processing Zones, Special Economic Zones and the Long March of Capitalist Development Policies During the Cold War." In *Decolonization and the Cold War: Negotiating Independence*, edited by Leslie James and Elisabeth Leake, 63–84. London: Bloomsbury, 2015.

Neveling, Patrick. "Free Trade Zones, Export Processing Zones, Special Economic Zones and Global Imperial Formations 200 BCE to 2015 CE." In *The Palgrave Encyclopedia of Imperialism and Anti-Imperialism*, edited by I. Iin Ness and Z. Cope, 1007–16. Basingstoke: Palgrave Macmillan, 2015.

"Not So Special." *The Economist,* April 4, 2015. https://www.economist.com/leaders/2015/04/04/not-so-special.

O'Brien, Matt. "The Miraculous Story of Iceland." *The Washington Post,* June 17, 2015. https://www.washingtonpost.com/news/wonk/wp/2015/06/17/the-miraculous-story-of-iceland/.

O'Carroll, Lisa. "Government Statement on the Announcement of Joint EU–IMF Programme for Ireland." *The Guardian,* November 28, 2010. https://www.theguardian.com/business/ireland-business-blog-with-lisa-ocarroll/2010/nov/28/ireland-bailout-full-government-statement.

O'Connell, Hugh. "Bertie Says Crisis Caused by 'Joe Soap and Mary Soap' Getting Too Many Loans." *The Journal,* December 14, 2015. https://www.thejournal.ie/bertie-ahern-joe-and-mary-soap-2501249-Dec2015/.

O'Donnell, Orla. "100,000 March against War in Iraq." *RTÉ Archives,* February 15, 2003. https://www.rte.ie/archives/2013/0215/367908-10-years-ago-today-protest-against-iraq-war/.

O'Driscoll, Dennis. *Collected Poems.* Manchester: Carcanet, 2017.

Óglaigh na hÉireann / Irish Defence Forces. "LÉ Samuel Beckett." *YouTube,* May 17, 2014. https://www.youtube.com/watch?v=npbglEGYRsI.

O'Halloran, Barry. "Deal with Chinese Province Guangdong Set to Boost Irish Trade." *The Irish Times,* June 9, 2017. https://www.irishtimes.com/business/transport-and-tourism/deal-with-chinese-province-guangdong-set-to-boost-irish-trade-1.3114319.

O'Hearn, Denis. *The Atlantic Economy: Britain, the US and Ireland.* Manchester: Manchester University Press, 2015.

O'Mahony, Niamh. "Introduction." In *Essays on the Poetry of Trevor Joyce,* edited by Niamh O'Mahony, 11–28. Bristol: Shearsman, 2015.

———, and Trevor Joyce. "Joyce in 2011: Finding a Language Use." *Jacket2,* February 3, 2014. https://jacket2.org/interviews/joyce-2011-finding-language-use.

Ong, Aihwa. "The Gender and Labor Politics of Postmodernity." *Annual Review of Anthropology* 20 (1991): 279–309. DOI: 10.1146/annurev.an.20.100191.001431.

Ó Riain, Seán. *The Rise and Fall of Ireland's Celtic Tiger: Liberalism, Boom and Bust.* Cambridge: Cambridge University Press, 2014.

O'Rourke, Kevin H., and Jeffrey G. Williamson. "When Did Globalization Begin?" In *European Review of Economic History* 6, no. 1 (2002): 23–50. DOI: 10.3386/w7632.

O'Toole, Fintan. "Liechtenstein on the Liffey: State Policy Has Turned Dublin into a Wild Frontier of Cooked Books and Dodgy Transactions." *The Guardian,* February 27, 2009. https://www.theguardian.com/commentisfree/2009/feb/27/liechenstein-liffey-tax-avoidance-dublin.

Owen, Stephen. *The Poetry of the Early Tang.* New Haven: Yale University Press, 1977.

"Political Priority, Economic Gamble." *The Economist,* April 4, 2015. https://www.economist.com/finance-and-economics/2015/04/04/political-priority-economic-gamble.

Powers, Harry S. "Mode and Raga." *The Musical Quarterly* 44, no. 4 (1958): 448–60. DOI: 10.1093/mq/XLIV.4.448.

Prynne, J.H. *Graft and Corruption: Shakespeare's Sonnet 15.* Cambridge: Face Press, 2016.

"Public Art: Per Cent for Art Scheme. General National Guidelines — 2004." 2004. https://publicart.ie/fileadmin/user_upload/PDF_Folder/Public_Art_Per_Cent_for_Art.pdf.

Rapp, Emily. "'The Spinning Heart' by Donal Ryan." *Boston Globe,* March 14, 2014. https://www.bostonglobe.com/arts/2014/03/14/book-review-the-spinning-heart-donal-ryan.

"Red Dust: The Capitalist Transition in China." *Chuǎng* 2 (2019): 21–281. https://chuangcn.org/journal/two/red-dust/.

Reddan, Fiona. *Ireland's IFSC: A Story of Global Financial Success.* Dublin: Mercier, 2008.

Reinares, Laura Barberan. "Globalized Philomels: State Patriarchy, Transnational Capital, and the Femicides on the US-Mexican Border in Roberto Bolano's *2666*." *South Atlantic Review* 75, no. 4 (2010): 51–72. DOI: 10.2307/41635653.

"Report of Department of Justice, Equality and Law Reform and An Garda Síochána Working Group on Trafficking in Human Beings." May 2006. https://www.legislationline.org/documents/id/5371.

Robertson, Roland. "Comments on the 'Global Triad' and 'Glocalization.'" In *Globalization and Indigenous Culture*, edited by Inoue Nobutaka, 217–26. Tokyo: Institute for Japanese Culture and Classics, Kokugakuin University, 1997.

Rodziński, Witold. *The Walled Kingdom*. Waukegan: Fontana, 1984.

Rollefson, J. Griffith. *Flip the Script: European Hip Hop and the Politics of Postcoloniality*. Chicago: University of Chicago Press, 2017.

Rusangano Family. "Artist Bio." https://web.archive.org/web/20160510161108/http://www.rusanganofamily.com/artist/bio.

———. "Lights On." *Rap Genius*. https://genius.com/Rusangano-family-lights-on-lyrics.

Ryan, Donal. *The Spinning Heart*. Dublin: Doubleday Ireland, 2012.

Samuel Beckett. *Worstward Ho*. In *Company/Ill Seen Ill Said/Worstward Ho/Stirrings Still*, edited by Dirk van Hulle, 79–103. London: Faber, 2009.

Sands, Anita. "The Irish Software Industry." In *From Underdogs to Tigers: The Rise and Growth of the Software Industry in Brazil, China, India, Ireland, and Israel*, edited by Ashish Arora and Alfonso Gambardella, 41–71. Oxford: Oxford University Press, 2005.

Sartis, Marthine. "Textual Voices of Irish History in Trevor Joyce's 'Trem Neul.'" In *Essays on the Poetry of Trevor Joyce*, edited by Niamh O'Mahony, 29–52. Bristol: Shearsman, 2015.

Scott, James C. *Against the Grain: A Deep History of the Earliest States*. New Haven: Yale University Press, 2017.

Shaughnessy, Edward. "The Religion of Ancient China." In *A Handbook of Ancient Religions,* edited by John R. Hinnells, 490–536. Cambridge: Cambridge University Press, 2007.

Sisson, Patrick. "The Small Irish Town That Inspired China's Free Trade Zones." *Curbed,* January 26, 2016. https://www.curbed.com/2016/1/26/10843212/shannon-ireland-shenzen-china-free-trade-zone.

Smith, Nicola Jo-Anne. *Showcasing Globalisation? The Political Economy of the Irish Republic.* Manchester: Manchester University Press, 2005.

"Sorghum & Steel: The Socialist Developmental Regime and the Forging of China." *Chuǎng* 1 (2016): 13–210. http://chuangcn.org/journal/one/sorghum-and-steel/.

"State Aid: Ireland Gave Illegal Tax Benefits to Apple Worth Up to €13 Billion." *European Comission.* http://europa.eu/rapid/press-release_IP-16-2923_en.htm.

Sutherland, Keston. *Hot White Andy.* Brighton: Barque, 2005.

Taylor, Catherine. "The Spinning Heart by Donal Ryan, Review." *The Telegraph,* August 8, 2013. https://www.telegraph.co.uk/culture/books/10218878/The-Spinning-Heart-by-Donal-Ryan-review.html.

"The Holding Pattern: The Ongoing Crisis and the Class Struggles of 2011–2013." *Endnotes* 3 (2013): 12–55. https://endnotes.org.uk/issues/3/en/endnotes-the-holding-pattern.

Twitchell-Waas, Jeffrey. "Twanging the Zither: Trevor Joyce and Chinese Poetry." In *Essays on the Poetry of Trevor Joyce,* edited Niamh O'Mahony, 195–218. Bristol: Shearsman, 2015.

"Union Challenges Production of Waterford Crystal in Slovenia." *The Irish Times,* March 5, 2013. https://www.irishtimes.com/business/manufacturing/union-challenges-production-of-waterford-crystal-in-slovenia-1.1317407.

van der Toorn, Karen. "The Public Image of the Widow in Ancient Israel." In *Between Poverty and the Pyre: Moments in the History of Widowhood,* edited by Jan Bremmer and Lourens Van Den Bosch, 19–30. London: Routledge, 2002.

van der Toorn, Karen. "Torn Between Vice and Virtue: Stereotypes of the Widow in Israel and Mesopotamia." In

Female Stereotypes in Religious Traditions, edited by Ria Kloppenborg and Wouter J. Hanegraaff, 1–13. Leiden: Brill, 1995.

Wang Yü-Ch'üan. "An Outline of The Central Government of The Former Han Dynasty." *Harvard Journal of Asiatic Studies* 12, nos. 1–2 (1949): 134–87. DOI: 10.2307/2718206.

Ward, Eilís. "Prostitution and the Irish State: From Prohibitionism to a Globalised Sex Trade." *Irish Political Studies* 25, no. 1 (2010): 47–65. DOI: 10.1080/07907180903431988.

Warriner, Rachel. *Eleven Days.* Cork: RunAmok, 2011.

"Was It for This?" *The Irish Times,* November 18, 2010. https://www.irishtimes.com/opinion/was-it-for-this-1.678424.

Wayman, Sheila. "As Employment Rights Change, Has the Au Pair Had Her Day?" *The Irish Times,* January 28, 2017. https://www.irishtimes.com/life-and-style/health-family/as-employment-rights-change-has-the-au-pair-had-her-day-1.2951047.

www.ingramcontent.com/pod-product-compliance
Lightning Source LLC
Chambersburg PA
CBHW071700170426
43195CB00039B/2402